# OUTLAW BIKERS AND THE MOB

"The Bloody Pact Between the Hells Angels and the Rizzuto Crime Family"

Nicholas Anthony Parisi

Copyright © 2025 by Nicholas A. Parisi
All rights reserved

All rights reserved. No part of this book may be reproduced, distributed, or transmitted in any form or by any means, including photocopying, recording, or other electronic or mechanical methods, without the prior written permission of the publisher, except in the case of brief quotations used in reviews, articles, or scholarly works.

Published by **Organized Crime Press**
www.AuthorNicholasParisi.com

ISBN- 979-8-9913436-1-0

Photo Insert Notes: All images in this book are authentic archival photographs, reproduced under fair use or licensed for publication. All trademarks and logos remain the property of their respective owners.

Cover by P. Lampridis, 52 Design Studios, Tavros, Greece

Printed in the United States of America

First Edition, 2025

# Disclaimer

This book is a work of nonfiction that examines the history and activities of organized crime and outlaw motorcycle clubs. It is an independent journalistic/educational work and is not affiliated with, sponsored by, or endorsed by the Hells Angels Motorcycle Club or any of its members.

The names **"Hells Angels"** and the **"death head" logo** are registered trademarks of the Hells Angels Motorcycle Club. Any use of these marks, including images reproduced within this book, is for editorial and informational purposes only, in connection with the discussion of the subject matter.

All trademarks, service marks, and logos remain the property of their respective owners.

# Before You Turn the Page...

Look, everything you're about to read? It's already out there. In the papers. On the evening news. In court transcripts, sworn testimony, and police files you could pull yourself if you knew the right clerk to ask.

This book doesn't spill any goddamn secrets. Nobody's breaking *omertà* here. No inside stuff, no club business, no family business. Every story in these pages is built from public records, media reports, and the kind of street legends that get whispered in bars and backrooms until they make their way into print.

And yeah, some of it's alleged, some of it's proven, and some of it's the kind of thing you couldn't prove if you had the gun, the body, and a nun for a witness. But it's all part of the history.

One more thing. I got nothing but the highest respect for the Rizzuto family, the Hells Angels Motorcycle Club, and anyone else whose name comes up in these pages. This isn't about disrespect. This is about telling the stories that have already been told, stories that built reputations, earned fear, and carved their place in the underworld's history books.

That's the deal. The rest? The REAL rest? That stays where it's always stayed. Out there, in the streets.

-Nick Parisi

# Introduction

Montreal was always a city of shadows. The cobblestones told stories, but the real power pulsed beneath in smoky backrooms, strip-club VIP lounges, and the hush of late-night meetings where names were never said out loud. This wasn't fiction. It wasn't a movie. This was the underworld's frontline, and for a time, it was ruled by an unholy alliance. The Sicilian Mafia and the Hells Angels Motorcycle Club.

On one side, the Rizzuto Crime Family, old-world *Cosa Nostra* royalty. They wore suits, not cuts. Their power wasn't loud. It whispered in boardrooms, at construction sites, in judges' offices. Vito Rizzuto was their king, calculating, ruthless, respected. He inherited Montreal like a mafia prince and ruled it like an emperor.

On the other, the Hells Angels, outlaws in leather, forged in rebellion and baptized in violence. They didn't ask permission. They took what they wanted with chrome pistols and fists wrapped in steel. They rode loud, moved fast, and didn't flinch. Under bosses like Maurice "Mom" Boucher, they became something more than a gang. They became an army.

And then they partnered up.

The mafia had the money, the political reach, the international connections. The bikers had the muscle, the street control, and the balls to do the dirty work. Together, they built a criminal empire that turned Montreal into a global smuggling hub. Cocaine, meth, hash, cash, guns, and women all flowing through the city's veins like blood in a wounded animal.

But power like that never holds.

This book is the story of their rise and their collapse. It's a tale of blood oaths, backroom deals, and betrayals in the dead of night. It's about sons who couldn't live up to their fathers. About killers who turned into businessmen, and businessmen who became butchers. It's about war, not in the jungles or deserts, but in cafés, parking lots, and quiet cul-de-sacs where car bombs and sniper fire replaced diplomacy.

You'll meet the men who ran it all.

Vito Rizzuto, the mob boss who kept peace with charm and fear. Mom Boucher, the biker general who started a war with the state. Leonardo Rizzuto, the lawyer who didn't want the throne, but took it anyway. And Marty Robert, the biker enforcer turned shot-caller, now threatening to rewrite the balance of power again.

This is a street-level retelling of a blood pact that once held Montreal's underworld in check and the violent unraveling that followed. You won't find good guys here, only survivors, ghosts, and predators circling the same carcass.

**This is the story of the Brotherhood.**
**And how it bled.**

## Table of Contents

The Birth of the Rizzuto Empire .................................................. 1

The Rise of the Canadian Hells Angels .................................. 19

The Fragile Alliance ........................................................................ 43

Business Over Blood ...................................................................... 55

The Golden Years ............................................................................ 67

Blood in the Shadows .................................................................... 83

The Fall of Vito Rizzuto .............................................................. 105

Law, Order, and Omertà ............................................................. 115

The Shot That Shook the Throne .............................................. 123

Photo Section ................................................................................. 137

Enter the Street Gangs ................................................................. 163

Fall of the Giants .......................................................................... 175

Vito Returns with Fire in His Eyes .......................................... 201

What Remains ............................................................................... 229

Headlines and Blood-Soaked Narratives ............................... 235

The Reluctant Prince ................................................................... 243

So, what now? ............................................................................... 265

About the Author ......................................................................... 269

# Part I: Origins of Power

# Chapter 1

# The Birth of the Rizzuto Empire

You gotta understand where this thing really starts. Not in some boardroom or marble-clad mansion. No. It starts on the dust-choked streets of Cattolica Eraclea, Sicily. Agrigento province. A place where goats outnumber cops, and the law doesn't come in a uniform, it comes in silence. Over there, a man's word is worth more than paperwork. And one sideways look? That could sign your death warrant.

That's where Nicolo Rizzuto was born, February 18, 1924. His old man, Vito Sr., had his feet in the fields and his fingers in things nobody talked about. Couple years earlier, he got nailed by an Italian military court for stealing from the army. That tells you something right there. This family wasn't built on fairy tales. And Nicolo's uncle, Calogero Renda, was a *campiere*, a Mafia taxman bleeding the farmers for tribute. So, yeah, Nicolo grew up in it. By the time he was a teenager, *omertà*, the code of silence, wasn't a lesson. It was a second language.

Then came the war. Sicily got bombed to hell. The place was rubble. No food, no work, no future.

But Nicolo? He wasn't sticking around, hustling lemons or running bootleg wine. He wanted more. In 1945, he married Libertina Manno. Her father, Antonio, was a local Mafioso boss. Nicolo didn't just marry a girl. He married into power. On February 21, 1954, with the island suffocating and opportunity shrinking, he packed up and got out. He had a wife, a kid named Vito, and a plan.

Next stop: Montreal, Quebec, Canada.

Montreal in the 1950s was a city split in half, half Catholic, half crooked. A place where the maple leaves were red, but the blood on the streets ran deeper.

Back then, the Cotroni family ran the show, controlling much of Montreal's drug trade. Calabrians. Vincenzo "Vic" Cotroni was the face, but his bulldog, Paolo Violi, was the teeth. They had New York's Bonannos behind them, which meant real clout.

Nicolo Rizzuto, being Sicilian, was treated like an outsider. A grunt, a peasant with manners. But what they didn't know was this. Nicolo was watching. Learning. Clocking every move.

He set up shop in Montreal's Italian neighborhoods, Little Italy, Saint-Léonard. Started pulling in Sicilians, many tied to clans back home, like the Cuntrera-Caruanas, who came from the same region in Sicily. His uncle, Antonio Manno, would later immigrate to Montreal as well in September 1964. Small-time stuff at first. Gambling. Smuggling. Construction side-hustles. He kept quiet, kept close to the people, and kept building. Where the Calabrians played the bully, Nicolo played the diplomat. He didn't need to bark. He just waited for the leash to snap. And eventually, it did.

By the '70s, that leash was breaking. The Cotronis were cracking like old pavement. The Calabrians ran the show, but the Sicilians, Nicolo's crew, led by Luigi Greco, were sick of playing second fiddle. This wasn't just business. It was blood politics. Sicily versus Calabria. Quiet patience versus loud noise.

And Violi? He had a mouth that wouldn't quit. Complained constantly about being a *decina*, a crew, under the Bonannos, wanted to break free, start his own family. What he didn't know was that the cops were listening, and those tapes? They didn't just end up in evidence lockers. They hit the streets.

In December 1970, Violi's office in the Reggio Bar in Montreal was bugged by an undercover policeman, Robert Ménard, who for the next five years recorded everything that Violi said in the Reggio Bar.

In December 1971, a meeting was called at a cottage outside of the village of L'Épiphanie to discuss the tensions between the Sicilian and Calabrian factions, with Violi representing the Calabrian faction while Leonardo Caruana, Giuseppe Cuffaro, and Pietro Sciara representing the Sicilian faction.

New York tried to mediate. In September 1972, Natale "Joe Diamond" Evole, the boss of the Bonanno family, sent wiseguys Nicky Alfano and Nicola Buttofuoco of New York to Montreal in an attempt to mediate the dispute. Ménard's bugs recorded Cotroni and Violi discuss "getting rid of" Rizzuto and making him "disappear" from the world forever. Giuseppe Settecase, a veteran Mafiosi with a criminal record going back to 1936, was sent north from New York in another attempt to mediate the dispute, which was threatening to break the Cotroni family apart. Settecase's attempt was no more successful, and instead, Cotroni and Violi asked him to take a message to "the *Commissione*," the governing board of the American Mafia, for permission to kill Rizzuto.

Tension then grew into a power struggle between the Calabrian and Sicilian factions of the family in 1973. Cotroni *Capodecina*, crew boss, Paolo Violi, complained about the independent means of his Sicilian 'underlings', Rizzuto in particular. "He is going from one side to the other, from Canada to the US and back, here and there, and he says nothing to nobody, he is doing business and nobody knows anything."

Violi asked for more soldiers from his Bonanno bosses, clearly preparing for war, and Violi's boss at the time, Vic Cotroni, remarked, "Me, I'm *Capodecina*. I got the right to expel." The request from Cotroni and Violi to "the Commission" to kill Rizzuto was refused. On the street, everyone knew Violi was running his mouth, and worse, that he didn't trust his own guys. And in this life, that's a death sentence.

From 1976 to 1980, Montreal turned into a shooting gallery.

The Rizzutos started picking off Violi's people one by one. First up, Pietro Sciara. The poor bastard walks out of a theater after seeing *The Godfather Part II*, boom, sawed-off shotgun to the head. Life imitating art. Then, Francesco Violi, the brother of Paolo, who had taken over as acting boss while he was imprisoned, was lined up against a wall and executed with a shotgun.

And Paolo himself? He gets out of Bordeaux prison in December '77 as he completed his sentence for contempt of the royal commission and became a marked man.

Less than a year later, Violi got whacked, shot in the head with a sawed-off shotgun outside his home. His brothers weren't far behind. Car bombs. Hit squads. The Calabrians crumbled, one bullet at a time. And when the smoke cleared, it wasn't Vic Cotroni sitting on the throne anymore. It was Nicolo Rizzuto.

But here's the thing, Nicolo was the foundation. The real story? His son. Vito Rizzuto.

Vito Rizzuto wasn't just another boss's kid. He was born for it. Handsome, educated, and sharper than a straight razor. He spoke French, Italian, and English like a native. He wasn't a street thug. He was a chess master in a room full of checkers players. Where Nicolo had laid the groundwork, Vito laid down the blueprints for a criminal empire.

He knew that violence had its place, but business came first. He cleaned up the family's image, traded the brass knuckles for cufflinks, and started moving pieces far beyond Montreal. He forged alliances with Sicilian heavyweights, the Inzerillos, the Cuntrera-Caruanas. He got in with South American coke cartels, with Mafia dons in New York, with muscle from the West End and finesse from the East. Though only considered a soldier of the New York Bonanno crime family by the Federal Bureau of Investigation, Rizzuto was considered by Canadian officials to be the most powerful mob boss in the country. Many experts consider the strength of the

Rizzuto clan to rival that of any of the Five Families in New York and dubbed it the "Sixth Family."

By the late '70s, the Rizzutos weren't just running Montreal, they were running a global pipeline. And you wanna know how Vito really took Montreal? It wasn't bullets. It was cement.

See, in the 1970s and '80s, the city was on the rise. Expo '67 had put Montreal on the map, and with the '76 Olympics coming, it turned into one giant construction site. Highways, tunnels, bridges, skyscrapers, everywhere you looked, there was rebar and wet concrete. Billions of dollars in contracts. And every one of those jobs was a payday waiting to happen. The problem was chaos. Labor unions were outta control, wildcat strikes, extortion, jobs being shut down over coffee breaks. It was a mess.

But Vito? He saw the mess as a ladder. And he climbed it.

First, he planted his guys inside the unions. The FTQ, CUQ names that made developers sweat. If you needed labor, you needed union. And if you needed union, you needed Vito. Period. His guys ran job sites like foremen with baseball bats. If a contractor played ball, they got peace. Those who didn't? Suddenly, cement trucks disappeared, machines "broke down," picket lines showed up overnight. And here's the beauty of it, he didn't need to threaten people. Just a whisper that "Mr. Rizzuto isn't happy," and people fell in line.

That influence flowed up the ladder fast. Developers wanted quiet, smooth builds. Politicians wanted votes and union donations. Vito gave them both. In return, his companies' legit fronts with dirty roots won contract after contract. Some worth tens of millions. Government-funded. Publicly celebrated. Privately skimmed.

It was the perfect storm of corruption, greed, and silence. And it made Vito rich. Not flashy-rich. Not gold-chain, pinky-ring rich. But invisible-rich. Offshore accounts. Construction firms in numbered companies. Restaurants and import/export fronts washing more cash than a laundromat on payday.

See, Vito understood something most wiseguys never got. Real power doesn't shout. It whispers. While bikers waved colors and street punks showed gold chains, Vito wore designer suits and silk ties. He shook hands with judges, had lunch with city officials, and dropped donations into political campaigns. You'd see him at charity dinners, sipping wine with the same people awarding his company contracts. He made himself indispensable. Politicians came to him when they needed help "motivating" certain voters. Inspectors turned a blind eye when his crews built without permits. In city hall, zoning laws bent like wet paper. His power was bureaucratic, subtle. But absolute.

You ever wondered how a construction bid twice the price still wins the contract?

That's Vito.

And the people loved him. In Little Italy, he was a godfather in the truest sense. Gave out turkeys at Christmas. Paid tuition for neighborhood kids. Made sure grannies got their meds and no one touched their shops. Even cops admitted, "He keeps the peace." Because Vito didn't just play the game, he owned the board.

Now, let's talk dope.

All that union money, all those construction rackets. That was the surface. But underneath? That's where the real cash flowed. And it flowed through the Port of Montreal. One of the busiest ports in North America, with thousands of containers coming in every week. Most clean. Some loaded with dope. And guess who controlled the offloading crews, the inspectors, the warehouses?

Vito.

Through his Sicilian connections, the Inzerillos, the Cuntrera-Caruanas, he got product straight from the source. Colombian coke. Heroin from the Golden Crescent. Containers filled with fruit that hid bricks of white gold. It came in quietly, got moved through stash houses across Canada and the U.S., and was sold by people who didn't even know who they were working for. Buffalo, Toronto, Detroit, New York. He had distribution hubs like a Fortune 500 logistics company. But this was no Amazon. This was Mafia Prime.

He didn't touch the street-level stuff. That was for soldiers, subcontractors, and street gangs paying tribute. Vito ran logistics and took a cut from everything. His crew didn't just get rich. They became the merchant bankers of the underworld.

And that money? It flowed right back into condos, construction, casinos, and politics. Clean, quiet, and unstoppable.

Now, you don't build an empire alone, not in this life. Especially not in the underworld. Vito might've been the face, the brain, and the boss, but behind him stood a small, deadly-efficient crew who kept the machine oiled, the money moving, and the bodies buried. These weren't yes-men. These were professionals. Men who bled the code, kept their mouths shut, and moved like ghosts through a city that never knew they were pulling the strings.

At the top of the pyramid stood Vito Rizzuto. "*Capo di Tutti Capi.*" The Boss of bosses. He didn't shout orders. He whispered them. But when Vito spoke, grown men listened like it was gospel. He was the architect, the diplomat, the Don. If something moved in Montreal's underworld from a kilo of coke at the port to a crooked union vote, it happened with his blessing.

Let's meet the bench.

Paolo Renda – The *Consigliere*. Advisor.

He wasn't the kind of man who raised his voice. He didn't carry a gun. He didn't need to.

Paolo Renda was the brains in the back room, the soft-spoken surgeon of power plays, and the last voice Vito Rizzuto heard before making a move. He was family, Vito's brother-in-law, but in the mob world, blood only got you so far. What made Renda indispensable wasn't the marriage. It was the mind. In a world of muscle and noise, Renda was a ghost. No flashy cars. No big entourage. Just a quiet suit, a briefcase, and a Rolodex filled with judges, union heads, and city bureaucrats who owed him more than favors.

He didn't run crews. He ran equations, laundering blueprints and risk assessments scribbled on the back of napkins in quiet corner booths. If Vito was the king, Renda was the prime minister, orchestrating moves behind velvet curtains. He knew where the bodies were buried, not because he put them there, but because he signed off on the hit and balanced the books afterward. His hands stayed clean, but they held the ledger on everyone else's dirt.

When heat came down on a racket, Renda called in a zoning board favor to make it disappear. When the unions got restless, he reminded their bosses who paid for their kids' tuition. He didn't threaten. He didn't scream. He just reminded. One phone call from Renda could cool down a street war or light the match on a political scandal. He didn't make scenes. He made things happen.

He was the type of man who sat silently in meetings, eyes half-lidded, absorbing every word. And when he finally spoke, everyone listened. Because Renda didn't waste breath. If he said a man had to go, that man was already dead. He just didn't know it yet. Police never caught him with a wiretap saying anything incriminating. He never raised a red flag. But if you zoomed out far enough over the drug routes, the unions, the political favors, the money trails, his fingerprints were everywhere.

You never saw him coming, but if you were lucky, he came instead of someone with a silencer.

Francesco Arcadi – *Sotto Capo*. Underboss.

Then came the Underboss, Francesco Arcadi. The execution arm. Vito's pit bull in a leather coat. Arcadi kept the engine running, coordinating crews, smoothing tensions, and making sure the street soldiers never forgot who they worked for. If Vito was the brain, Arcadi was the fists.

Arcadi was old school. Hard-faced, no-nonsense, the kind of guy who didn't speak unless something needed to be done, and when he spoke, people listened. As a Calabrian, Arcadi was an outsider in the Sicilian Rizzuto family whose leaders almost all came from the villages of Cattolica Eraclea and Siculiana. Despite being a Calabrian, Arcadi was very close to Rizzuto, with whom he normally went on vacations with to the Dominican Republic every January.

Within the Rizzuto family, Arcadi was known as "Compare Frank". He was Vito's enforcer-turned-interim boss when the Don got pinched and sent south.

He wasn't flashy, and that's what made him dangerous. Arcadi handled the daily grind. Disputes, discipline, and diplomacy. He didn't just run soldiers, he shaped them. Taught them the codes. No mess, no noise, no freelancing.

Rocco Sollecito – *Caporegime*. Crew Boss.

Below the underboss were the *Caporegimes*, or *Capos*. Men like Stefano "Rocco" Sollecito ran their own crews with regional authority. They were middle management with murder on speed dial. Each *Capo* controlled slices of turf. Montreal North, Laval, Saint-Leonard, even Ottawa and Toronto pipelines. They oversaw loansharking, protection rackets, gambling dens, construction kickbacks, and cocaine sales. They weren't just enforcers. They were franchise owners, keeping the brand strong while kicking a cut upstairs. And if they didn't? A closed casket funeral followed.

Rocco was the velvet glove over the brass knuckles. Charismatic, smooth, and meticulous, he was the guy Vito sent to make peace or to warn that peace was over. He wasn't just a fixer. He was the architect of deals. Drugs, alliances, truces. And when things went sideways, he didn't panic. He recalculated. Street guys respected him because he never acted bigger than them. But make no mistake, Sollecito could call in a hit with the flick of a cigarette.

He held the city's pulse and knew when it skipped a beat.

Raynald Desjardins – The Outsider Who Got In

Now here's where it gets interesting. Raynald was French-Canadian, an outsider in a business that didn't exactly open its arms to non-Italians. But Desjardins wasn't just anybody. He was sharp, ruthless, and had deep connections in Quebec's construction and biker scenes. Vito brought him in because he knew the value of someone who spoke both the street and the suite. Desjardins had the clout to bring rival factions to the table and the muscle to flip it when needed. He helped expand the Rizzuto empire beyond the Italian sphere, striking quiet partnerships with Hells Angels and politically connected business types. But power makes people dream of the throne.

The *Soldati*, Soldiers.

Enforcers and Earners. *Affranchi*. Made men. Initiated into the life. You didn't get to this level without proving your loyalty and your capacity for violence. They were the guys who handled the collections, shook down deadbeats, protected the drug mules, and made sure witnesses disappeared or changed their stories before trial. They walked the line between criminal and civilian, fear and favor. They wore Rolexes and gold rings but carried knives behind their backs. You didn't mess with soldiers. You paid them. Or you paid for it.

The Associates.

Grease for the Gears. Not all the players wore a pinky ring. Associates were the outer shell. Not made men, but useful stand-up guys. Bikers, street gang captains, union reps, nightclub owners, real estate brokers, airport workers, corrupt port officials, even the odd city councilman with a gambling problem. They were valuable because of what they could do, not who they were. Some provided muscle. Others cleaned cash. Some fixed permits, stuffed ballot boxes, or helped smuggle coke through cargo containers labeled as frozen fish. They weren't family. But if they delivered? They were protected.

Now, don't mistake them for a crew of thugs or street-level toughs. The Rizzuto Organization was a machine greased by blood, built on silence, and run like a Fortune 500 company with a Sicilian playbook. They weren't a gang. They were a shadow government. And in Montreal, they ruled without needing a crown. This wasn't chaos. It was structure. Loyalty was law. Money was religion. Orders flowed down. Money flowed up. If you earned, you ate. If you caused heat, you vanished. The system rewarded loyalty and punished ambition without permission. Nobody freelanced. Nobody made a move without clearing it. It was a hierarchy of silence, soaked in tradition. And when everyone played their part? It ran like an invisible empire hiding in plain sight.

Vito was Sicilian, sure. But his mind was bigger than bloodlines. He brought in Irish muscle, Jewish fixers, Haitian street contacts, and French-Canadian logisticians. He treated crime like a business, and business didn't care about ethnicity, just results. That's what made his empire so damn durable. While other crews fell apart over tradition and territory, the Rizzutos flexed, adapted, and kept growing. Like a corporation with brass knuckles with a priest on retainer.

By the early '80s, the groundwork was done. The Cotronis were sidelined, the Calabrians crushed, and Montreal? It was stitched into the Rizzuto family's tailored suit.

But Vito wasn't in the game for nickels and dimes. He wasn't satisfied with being king of one city. He wanted to run an empire. And to build an empire, you need three things: product, logistics, and protection. He had all three, and he used Montreal like a launchpad into the global underworld.

You want to understand how drugs flood a country? Follow the docks.

The Port of Montreal was a gift wrapped in concrete. Busy, chaotic, under-secured, perfect for slipping in multi-ton shipments of coke and heroin. The Rizzutos knew it, and so did their friends across the ocean. Vito leaned heavily on his Sicilian roots. He reconnected with the Cuntrera-Caruana clan, the so-called "Rothschilds of the Mafia." These guys were white-collar Narcos, accountants with bulletproof briefcases, managing drug routes like Wall Street traders.

Through them, Vito got ties to the Inzerillo family in Palermo, who were themselves deep in the heroin pipeline that ran from *Türkiye* through Italy into the West. Add some Colombian suppliers into that mix, likely courtesy of cartel middlemen in Caracas and Panama, and the Rizzutos became a key player in the global coke trade.

Montreal was the gateway. Once the bricks landed, they'd move by truck or rail to Toronto, Vancouver, Winnipeg, down into Buffalo, Detroit, even New York. Vito's reach was long, and his crews were efficient. No street-corner dealing, no messy turf wars. This was wholesale trafficking, the Costco of blow, and business was booming. You can't move weight like that without a tight supply chain. Vito ran his like FedEx With Guns.

He used shell companies in import/export, warehousing, and transportation. The trucks were clean on the outside, but on the inside? False floors, hidden compartments, heat-sealed kilos stacked like firewood. Crews rotated routes. Drivers were paid to keep quiet. If one got caught, the lawyers were already on speed dial. Everything was compartmentalized. One crew moved it. Another stored it. A third handled sales and distribution. Nobody knew more than they had to, and everyone kicked up to the boss. That's why the cops couldn't touch him. By the time they got a name, the drugs were already gone. And when you make that kind of cash, you gotta clean it. And Vito was a master cleaner.

Construction was the anchor, still rigging bids, still leaning on unions, but the empire had expanded. Restaurants. Real estate. Nightclubs. A few travel agencies that never booked a single flight. Vito funneled dirty money into legit businesses, then paid taxes on the clean end. It looked kosher, it smelled legal.

But it wasn't just Canada. Offshore accounts popped up in Panama, the Caymans, Zurich. Paper trails disappeared like ghosts. Paolo Renda oversaw most of the laundering, flipping bricks of cash into wires, investments, and silent partnerships in everything from condos to casinos. It was laundering as art. And the government? They didn't even know what to look for.

The Rizzuto name carried weight in Canada. But Vito wanted global clout. So, he built bridges sometimes with blood, sometimes with bourbon.

In New York, he had deep ties to the Bonanno crime family, his original American sponsor. In 1981, he even flew down to help take out three rival Bonanno *Capos*, Al "Sonny Red" Indelicato, Philip "Lucky" Giaccone, and Dominick "Big

Trin" Trinchera. A hit like that? That's not just muscle, that's diplomacy. It made Vito a player on U.S. soil.

Back in Italy, his Sicilian ties never faded. He was seen as the Canadian branch of *Cosa Nostra*. When the old country needed muscle or a safe haven, Vito opened his doors. In return, he got dope, leverage, and a piece of the European pie.

Down in South America, his alliances with importers and fixers in Venezuela and Colombia kept the product flowing. The port was open, the cops were paid, and the containers rolled in under the nose of customs.

What made it all work? Respect.

Vito didn't strong-arm people. He made them offers they wanted to say yes to. He was a negotiator, a connector. In a business full of hotheads, he was ice cold. While all this global expansion was happening, Vito never lost grip on the streets. He wasn't into bloodbaths. He wasn't like the old Calabrians who'd leave bodies in bars to send a message. Vito believed in whispers. You got one warning. Disobey, disrespect, or deviate from the rules, and you vanished.

His enforcer crews, run by guys like Arcadi and Sollecito, kept the peace with surgical precision. Meetings were held in safe houses, never on phones. Code words were gospel. New recruits were vetted harder than cops run background checks. Loyalty wasn't optional. It was currency. And for those who stayed in line? You ate good. You dressed clean. You got rich. That's why guys followed Vito. Not just because he was the boss, but because under his rule, things worked.

By the end of the '80s, Vito wasn't just a mafia boss. He was a global brand. He had made Montreal a hub in the world's underground economy. He had pulled together Sicilian traditionalists, French-Canadian opportunists, and international traffickers into one smooth-running machine. Lawyers, cops, and politicians either feared him, owed him, or didn't even know he was there. That's power. The quiet kind. The kind that doesn't need to shout. But power comes with heat. And the more Vito built, the more enemies he made.

By the early '90s, the Rizzuto empire purred like a tuned-up Cadillac. Smooth, quiet, dangerous under the hood. Vito had everything locked down. Montreal was his, the ports were his, the unions were his. But more than that, the game was his. No loud shootouts. No public bloodbaths. Just profit. Quiet dominance. Politicians took meetings. Cops looked the other way. Rivals either kicked up, shut up, or disappeared. Even the Hells Angels respected the balance. But when the streets are too quiet? That's when you start listening for footsteps. And down in Brooklyn, the past was starting to knock.

Let's rewind for a second.

In the summer of '81, New York's Bonanno family was a war zone. Three rebel *Capos*, "Sonny Red" Indelicato, "Big Trin" Trinchera, and "Lucky" Giaccone, were plotting to overthrow boss Philip Rastelli and his man on the street, Joseph Massino.

You remember *Donnie Brasco*? Well, the street didn't roll credits. It kept going.

Massino, a savvy operator, smelled the betrayal. And instead of waiting for war, he called for preemptive murder.

Enter Vito. He wasn't even American-born. He had no legal status in the U.S., just ties to the Bonannos through his old man and years of quiet business with Massino. But when the call came, Vito got on a plane. Because loyalty, in this life, ain't optional. He joined the crew at a social club in Queens.

The three rebel capos were invited to a sit-down. The second they walked in, boom. Execution-style hits. Fast, brutal, efficient. Blood soaked the carpet. One body, Sonny Red's, was buried in a lot in Ozone Park, discovered 23 years later by accident. The others? Dumped and forgotten.

It was Vito's first major step onto the American stage. And it showed something deeper. That he wasn't just a Canadian boss. He was a Mafia ambassador. A man who could cross borders and kill with impunity. But blood leaves stains. And some stains don't fade.

Back in Brooklyn, things were changing. Joseph Massino had climbed to the top of the Bonanno family. And for a while, he ruled with an iron hand. But law enforcement in the U.S. was getting smarter. More surveillance. Better RICO tactics. Witness protection deals that made rats out of made men.

And just like that, the biggest domino toppled.

In 2003, Massino was arrested on a slew of charges. Racketeering, murder, extortion. Facing life, he did the unthinkable. He flipped. First Five Families boss ever to rat. And guess what he gave them?

Everything. Including Vito.

That 1981 triple murder, buried in blood and silence for over 20 years, was back on the table. And this time, they had names, details, dates. Enough to draw a direct line from Brooklyn to Montreal. Suddenly, the "Teflon Don of Canada" had a warrant on his back.

Before the papers even landed, the squeeze was on. The walls held, but the cracks were showing.

# Chapter 2

# The Rise of the Canadian Hells Angels

Lemme tell you how Montreal was back then. On one side, you had the Rizzutos, slick Sicilian dons in silk ties, moving containers of coke through the port like it was Amazon Prime. Smooth. Quiet. Respectable. At least if you didn't look too close. And on the other side? You had the Hells Angels, better known in Quebec as *"Les Hells."* No silk ties, no subtle smiles. Just Harleys, patches, and a middle finger the size of a freight train.

If the Mafia ran the city like chess masters, the Angels stormed through it like a wrecking crew. And together? Forget about it. That's how Montreal became the black heart of Canada.

This wasn't a story of accidental expansion or wild youth gone off the rails. It was conquest, bloody, deliberate, and organized. It didn't start in Montreal, though.

You wanna talk Angels, you gotta go back to California. Post-WWII, late '40s. Picture this. Vets coming home from the Pacific, half-crazy from what they'd seen, the suburbs too quiet, too clean. The factories bored 'em, the nine-to-five was a joke. These guys needed adrenaline, brotherhood, something that felt like combat again. So, they built their own army. Only this one ran on chrome and gas instead of boots and bullets. They didn't wear rings of gold. They wore vests patched with death's head.

It started on March 17, 1948, in Fontana, California, when several small motorcycle clubs agreed to merge. Otto Friedli, a World War II veteran, is credited with starting the club after breaking from the Pissed Off Bastards motorcycle club over a feud with a rival gang. They called themselves the Hells Angels, reportedly borrowing the name from a World War II squadron of the 303rd Bombardment Group. Perfect. These weren't choirboys. These were men wired for violence, allergic to rules, who wanted freedom at 120 miles an hour.

The club's first official charter was reportedly hammered out in 1950, more tattoo parlor than boardroom, more bar napkin than bylaw. But it didn't matter. The spirit was there. Ride hard, live free, take no shit. And just like that, the Hells Angels were born not as a monolith, but as a wildfire spreading from engine to engine.

By the early 1950s, California was fertile ground for outlaws. Returning vets on the fringe of society gravitated to the open roads and open bottles, looking for meaning in speed and madness. As riders moved from town to town, they took the legend with them. No cell phones. No websites. Just stories and scars. And with each relocation came new roots.

In 1954, down in the smog and strut of San Francisco, a new chapter lit up. The Frisco charter, as it came to be known, rose from the ashes of the Market Street Commandos, a wild bunch with a reputation for living fast and falling harder. These weren't wannabe rebels. They were ex-fighters, ex-cons, and ex-everythings men who didn't fit into the clean postwar suburban dream.

By 1956, the movement had rolled north, with a North Sacramento chapter forming in the capital's rougher corners. It wasn't long before two brothers, James "Mother" Miles and Pat Miles, broke off to start another charter nearby. These weren't your average Sunday riders. They were former Hell Bent for Glory members, a crew known more for their brawls than their brotherhood. The Miles brothers had fire in their guts and oil in their veins, and they weren't interested in asking permission.

Their Sacramento charter would eventually burn out, the club fragmenting under internal tensions and external heat. But the embers didn't die, they just moved. In 1965, the remnants relocated to Richmond and rebranded as a Nomads chapter, unbound by geography, untethered from any single city. They would ride wherever the road and the business took them.

But if you're talking about the man who gave this chaos structure, who forged myth into machine, you have to talk about Ralph "Sonny" Barger.

In 1957, Sonny Barger founded the Oakland charter. That's the game-changer. Barger wasn't just a biker. He was a general. A born leader with ice in his stare and asphalt in his soul. And he organized. He understood that a scattered brotherhood was a vulnerable one. So, he began to unify the fractured landscape. According to Barger, other charters had sprouted up in places like Gardena and North Chino/South Pomona, often completely unaware that other Angels even existed. It was a decentralized rebellion. But Barger brought order to the anarchy. Common bylaws. Shared patches. A single flag flying over many fires. He turned a wild mosaic of riders into a brand and an outlaw institution that would one day span continents.

By the late 1960s, even the more obscure charters, like the one in North Chino and South Pomona, had earned their place in the growing legend. While they never made headlines like Oakland or San Bernardino, known as Berdoo, they helped keep the culture alive. Bar fights, drug runs, backroad rides, and all.

The Hells Angels weren't born overnight. They were forged in a thousand barrooms, across a thousand miles, by men who didn't give a damn about rules unless they were their own. What began as scattered sparks across California became a firestorm. And by the time law enforcement started paying attention, it was too late. You didn't just wear the patch. You earned it. And once you had it?

You lived and died for it.

Through the 1960s and '70s, they became counterculture icons and police punching bags, menacing longhairs in leather who'd show up at rock concerts, bar fights, and funerals. But under the smoke of the media circus, the Angels were getting organized. Cocaine was coming in. Guns were going out. They had structure, ranks, and bylaws. The freewheeling rebels were becoming a criminal enterprise.

Before the Angels were cutting deals with Sicilian dons in Montreal, they were already written into America's criminal folklore, and one night in 1969 burned their name into pop culture forever.

December 6, Altamont Speedway, California. The Rolling Stones wanted their own Woodstock, a free festival, West Coast style. The problem? They didn't hire security. Instead, they cut a deal with the Hells Angels, $500 worth of beer to keep the peace. That's right, beer, not cash.

That was the first mistake.

The Angels rolled in on their Harleys and lined them up at the front of the stage like a chrome-and-steel wall. They weren't there to hold hands and hum along. They were there to guard the band with pool cues, chains, and the kind of glares that could freeze a man mid-step. From the first act, it was chaos. Three hundred thousand people packed into a racetrack that couldn't handle half that number. Bad acid was circulating. The crowd was surging forward, pressing into the bikes, the Angels swinging hard on anyone who got too close.

By sunset, the air was boiling. Then, during *"Under My Thumb,"* it happened. Eighteen-year-old Meredith Hunter, in a lime-green suit, got into it with the Angels. Shoved hard, he pulled a pistol. An Angel named Alan Passaro lunged, stabbing him twice. The knife flashed in the stage lights. Hunter dropped. He didn't get back up. The band played on. Maybe they didn't see it. Maybe they didn't want to. But the cameras did. The killing is immortalized in *Gimme Shelter*. What was meant to be a crown jewel of the hippie movement became the final blaze of the peace-and-love generation.

That night changed the Hells Angels' reputation forever. To the public, they weren't just bikers anymore. They were the dark side of the counterculture. Men who didn't follow rules, didn't play for the cameras, and sure as hell didn't care about peace-and-love speeches. Altamont had shown the world the Angels could turn a stage into a war zone.

In Montreal, they'd prove they could do the same to a city.

Canada wasn't just a new frontier. It was a powder keg waiting for a spark, and in 1977, the Hells Angels lit the match. They didn't sneak across the border. They detonated onto the scene by patching over the Popeyes Motorcycle Club, Quebec's most feared biker gang. Before the Angels ever flew the death head over Montreal, the Popeyes ruled the streets savage, unhinged, and dripping in menace. They took their name from a cartoon, but there was nothing animated about the carnage they unleashed.

In the back alleys of 1960s and '70s Montreal, the Popeyes were kings not because anyone loved them, but because no one dared to challenge them. They were denim-and-leather butchers, wielding chains, bats, and rage. At their peak, they were the second-largest biker crew in Canada, behind only Satan's Choice. When the Hells Angels took them in, they weren't just gaining numbers. They were inheriting chaos with a taste for blood. Their rep was soaked in blood and adrenaline, exactly the kind of chaos the Angels needed if they wanted to make a real move north of the border.

Walking into a Popeyes bar with the wrong jacket was like walking into church with a pentagram tattooed on your forehead. You weren't walking out the same.

It wasn't enough to make you strip your cut, your patched leather vest. They made a scene out of it. They'd roll up on rival riders like hyenas, beat them down, rip the patches off their fucking backs, and parade the spoils like trophies. Entire vests were nailed to the walls of their clubhouse, a sick museum of humiliation, meant to send a message to every other crew in the province. This is Popeyes turf. You don't fly our colors unless you bleed for them. That brutal pride, that aggressive self-policing of symbolism, made them infamous. But it also made them useful.

By the early 1970s, the Popeyes weren't just loud, they were lethal for hire. They started doing enforcement for the Dubois Brothers, a ruthless French-Canadian crime family that controlled gambling, loansharking, and drug turf across Montreal. The Popeyes weren't brought in for their charm. They were there to settle debts with boots and bullets.

Need a dealer straightened out? Popeyes.

Need a rival scared off? Popeyes.

Need someone erased? Popeyes.

They were blunt instruments, and the Dubois swung them hard.

But muscle gets hungry. After a while, the Popeyes weren't satisfied being the Dubois' pit bulls. They wanted their own piece. So, they started slinging dope themselves. Speed, smack, coke. They were violent entrepreneurs in an outlaw economy. No rules. No apologies. No limits. And with guys like Yves "Apache" Trudeau in their ranks, they had the deadliest insurance policy you could imagine.

Trudeau didn't look like a killer. At 22, he was unassuming, almost forgettable. But inside him boiled a calm, cold engine of death.

In the early 1970s, he joined the East End chapter of the Popeyes. It was the start of one of the most prolific murder careers in Canadian history. Trudeau wasn't just a hitman. He made people disappear. A mechanic of execution. He killed not for thrills, but for duty. Methodical. Controlled. Efficient. Over the years, as the Popeyes were absorbed into the Hells

Angels, Trudeau followed the patch trading one bloodstained brotherhood for another.

By the time he was done, over 40 bodies lay in his wake. Some were bikers, some were rivals, some were just in the way. Bombs, bullets, blades, Trudeau was a student of all. He eventually earned a new name. "The Killer with the Baby Face."

By the mid-1970s, the Popeyes had carved out a place in Montreal's criminal food chain. But their savagery had made them difficult to control. The Hells Angels, looking to expand into Quebec, saw an opportunity. Instead of fighting them, why not bring the dogs inside the house?

In '77, the Hells Angels swallowed up the Popeyes in a violent collision. American outlaw structure crashing head-on with French-Canadian biker savagery. The east-end Popeyes flipped their patches and became the first Hells Angels charter in Canada. In Quebec, nobody bothered with the full name. They were just *Les Hells*. A match made in hell, and from that day on, the face of organized crime in Canada was never the same.

The Popeyes weren't just tough. They were vicious. These were street soldiers who stabbed first and asked questions never. Their business was drugs, intimidation, enforcement. They didn't need a rebrand, but when the offer came from the Hells Angels, backed by American clout and a promise of an empire, they saw what it was. An invitation to the majors. That handshake deal, inked in blood, bullets, and biker respect, was the birth of the Canadian Hells Angels.

And Montreal? That became their stomping ground.

From the start, *Les Hells* weren't playing small. They didn't ride around for bar fights and badge-baiting anymore. This was business. Drugs. Arms. Protection. Montreal's underworld, already tangled with Mafia turf wars and street gang rivalries, was the perfect storm. And *Les Hells* were the thunder. They absorbed or wiped out local biker outfits like parasites in leather. They created "support clubs" to do their dirty work, guys who'd never wear the full patch but would kill for the chance. Every block they took was soaked in sweat and blood. Every new chapter was a foothold in a national takeover.

Now, every empire needs a face, and for the Canadian Angels, it was Maurice "Mom" Boucher.

Boucher looked like a retired linebacker, spoke like a preacher with a switchblade, and ruled like a king with a god complex. Boucher wasn't born to follow. He was born to burn down the old ways. Before he was the face of terror in Quebec's underworld, before the bloodbaths and biker wars, Mom Boucher was just another angry, muscle-bound thug with a chip on his shoulder and a taste for power. He didn't come from Mafia stock or old-world tradition. He came from the cracked pavement of Pointe-aux-Trembles, the rough eastern tip of Montreal, an industrial, working-class neighborhood where fists settled most disputes, and a sense of belonging was found behind handlebars, not family dinners.

In the early 1980s, Boucher ran with a homegrown white supremacist biker gang known as the SS. Real scumbags. Beating up immigrants and smashing shops. Racist trash. But even there, Boucher stood out. Big, charismatic, mean. He and his buddy Sal Cazzetta ran the show, a pair of ambitious bruisers with a hunger for more than just hate crimes and bar brawls.

Enter Normand "Biff" Hamel, another SS original, a street dealer with a sharper eye for business.

While Boucher and the crew were out cracking skulls, Hamel was already knee-deep in the drug game. He pitched a new direction for the gang. Less ideology, more income. As Hamel put it, "Beating up immigrants might be fun, but it doesn't pay." Coke, hash, pills, that's where the money was.

The SS, thanks to Hamel's influence, started shifting from racist thugs to criminal entrepreneurs. And as the violence turned profitable, bigger players started to notice, including the Hells Angels, who had recently made their first bloody mark in Quebec by absorbing the Popeyes MC. Boucher and Cazzetta were now on the radar.

In 1984, everything stopped for a moment. That September, Boucher, then in his early twenties, crossed a line even the underworld doesn't always forgive. He held a gun to the head of a 16-year-old girl, threatening to kill her unless she had sex with him. It wasn't a rumor or an accusation. It was a conviction. He went down for armed sexual assault and did 40 months in prison.

But even locked up, Boucher kept hustling. Get this, he worked the unemployment system, had the checks mailed straight to the prison. It wasn't until a sharp-eyed clerk flagged the address as a correctional facility that the payments were cut off nearly three years later.

When he got out in January 1986, Boucher wasted no time. The SS was done. The new play was power, and the path to it was wearing the iconic Death Head patch of the Hells Angels. He joined the Montreal chapter, sponsored by none other than Biff Hamel, his old SS comrade and now a fully patched

Angel. Within months, Boucher proved himself worthy, vicious, loyal, and absolutely fearless.

Then came May 1, 1987. Just three days after Martin Huneault, the leader of the rival Death Riders, was shot dead in a Laval bar while watching a hockey game, Mom Boucher became a full-patch Hells Angel.

The timing was no coincidence. The hit on Huneault wasn't messy. It was military. The shooter walked into the bar, three rounds, cold and clean, then disappeared. There were plenty of witnesses, but no one said a word. Not one soul testified that Boucher pulled the trigger, but everyone knew who did. Huneault had resisted bending the knee. He didn't want the Death Riders answering to the Hells Angels. That made him a problem. After his murder, the Death Riders folded into line and became a puppet club. The Angels now owned Laval's drug trade.

Mom Boucher's transformation from hate-fueled street thug to rising star in the most dangerous outlaw motorcycle club in Canada was complete. He had the patch, the body count, and the street cred. But more than that, he had ambition.

What came next would be darker than anything Quebec's underworld had seen. Bombings, mass murder, civil war in the biker ranks, and the public unraveling of a man who wanted to be king. He joined *Les Hells* and never looked back, rising through the ranks with a mix of charisma, brutality, and strategic genius. He didn't just want power. He wanted total control. He built the Nomads chapter in Quebec, a paramilitary death squad within the Hells Angels, free from territorial duties and laser-focused on one mission. Destroy all rivals. No rules. No borders. Just domination. And his prime target? The Rock Machine, a rival biker gang who dared to challenge the Angels' grip on Quebec's drug trade.

The 1990s in Quebec didn't feel like Canada. They felt like Medellín with frostbite. Boucher wanted monopoly, not rivalry. The Rock Machine wanted independence, not orders. And what began as territorial scuffles turned into a full-blown urban war, bombs on sidewalks, bullets in barrooms, and corpses stacked like firewood in alleyways. The streets of Montreal were shifting again. The old codes were cracking, the alliances fraying, and in the dark corners of the city, a war was brewing, one that would bathe Quebec in blood for nearly a decade.

At the center of it all stood Mom, no longer just a patched Hells Angel, but now the president of the Montreal chapter, and a man with a vision as ruthless as it was ambitious. He didn't just want territory. He wanted a monopoly. A total stranglehold on Quebec's lucrative street-level drug trade, from the slums of Hochelaga to the bars of Quebec City.

The Rock Machine wasn't as polished as the Angels, but they were no pushovers. Formed by his old friend-turned-rival Salvatore Cazzetta, the Rock Machine had carved out serious turf, controlling bars, street crews, and independent coke routes across Montreal's east end. For a while, there was balance. A cold tension, yes, but balance.

Then, June 1994. The balance shattered. Cazzetta got pinched. Two hundred kilos of cocaine. That's 440 pounds of pure, powdered power. Cazzetta was arrested for trying to bring it into Canada from the United States. It was the kind of bust that didn't just rattle a gang, it ripped the head off the beast. The Rock Machine was leaderless, off-balance, and vulnerable. Boucher saw his moment. With Cazzetta gone,

Boucher didn't hesitate. He wasn't about to let the Rock Machine reorganize or elect a new boss. He ordered the engines started. He wanted the streets, and he was ready to take them by force.

His first move? Deploy the Evil Ones and the Rockers, two vicious puppet clubs loyal to the Hells Angels. These weren't weekend bikers. They were street soldiers, loyal, low-profile, and ready to kill on command. Their job was simple. Start squeezing the bars, dealers, and corners held by the Rock Machine. No negotiations. No warnings. Take it or die.

Boucher began making his presence felt. He'd show up at Rock Machine-controlled bars in his leather cut, flanked by Angels and Rockers, and make it plain, "You can keep selling… but you're selling for us now." Some dealers flipped. They knew better than to play chicken with a monster like Boucher. But others held firm, loyal to the Rock Machine, or just too proud to bend the knee.

That pride would cost them everything.

On a humid summer afternoon, July 14, 1994, in downtown Montreal, two members of the Rockers, the Angels' most trusted puppets, walked into a motorcycle shop. Their target was a Rock Machine associate, just doing business, likely unaware that the war had already begun. They didn't talk. They didn't threaten. They just opened fire. Gunshots echoed through the shop like a drumroll of war. The associate went down in a puddle of blood and bullet casings. The shooters walked out like they owned the city. That was the moment. The spark. The fuse that lit the powder keg.

That's the opening bell. From '94 to '02, over 160 dead. It was a campaign of terror with no off switch, executed with military precision and medieval cruelty. Drive-bys, car bombs, daytime assassinations. They didn't care if you were a rival biker, a police informant, or an innocent bystander.

When 11-year-old Daniel Desrochers, playing in a nearby schoolyard, was blown apart by a Jeep wired with a remote-controlled bomb exploded meant for a Rock Machine target in 1995. That shook the city, but it didn't stop the blood. For Boucher, fear was the point. The more people panicked, the stronger the Angels looked.

Behind the war machine was the Nomads, Mom's elite death squad. These weren't weekend warriors. They were professional killers, unpatched to avoid easy identification, trained to operate like black-ops units. They scoped targets, planned routes, even rehearsed getaways. Most of them weren't drug dealers. They were enforcers, pure muscle and malice. Tucked in the industrial backstreets of East Montreal, in the long concrete shadow of the Olympic Stadium, stood a building that didn't advertise what it was, but everyone in the game knew. The squat, nondescript structure on Bennett Street was the beating heart of biker power in Quebec, the clubhouse of the Nomads chapter.

Just blocks from the clubhouse was Pro-Gym, Mom's favorite iron temple, a sprawling gym complex where juiced-up weightlifters and bikers sweated, plotted, and built bodies like machines. That place wasn't just where Boucher trained. It was where deals were whispered in locker rooms and beefs were settled with stares. Bennett Street and Pro-Gym formed a kind of biker Vatican, a sacred zone where power, muscle, and fear all converged.

From inside the Nomads' fortified clubhouse, Canada's cocaine trade was quietly centralized. While street gangs fought over crumbs and indie pushers hustled for ounces, they dealt in shipments the size of shipping containers. One thousand kilos at a time. That's what the Nomads bought, 1,000 kilos of South American powder per transaction. Enough to turn a small nation into a cokehead's paradise. Enough to flood every city in Canada twice over. The coke would arrive through the port, get split up, stepped on, and sent down the pipeline, with profits laundered through clubs, businesses, and offshore accounts.

Their sources? The Rizzuto crime family, Montreal's Sicilian mafia empire, and the legendary West End Gang, the Irish mob lords who controlled the Port of Montreal like it was their own personal vault.

But here's the twist, they didn't just buy for themselves. Boucher's Nomads operated like a biker cartel HQ. Every single Hells Angels chapter in Canada, whether in Halifax, Saskatoon, Vancouver, or Quebec City, was under strict marching orders. "You buy your product from the Nomads or you don't buy at all." That meant total control. No freelance hustling. No side deals. No unapproved suppliers. If you were a Hells Angel in Canada, your coke came through Bennett Street whether you liked it or not. And if you crossed the rule, if you tried to deal on the side or bring in your own shipments? You were either sidelined, stripped of your patch, or ended up a body in a ditch with your bike torched for the message.

The Angels waged a war of attrition. They didn't win with single battles. They won by making the cost of resistance too high. One Rock Machine member who defected to the Bandidos later described the war bluntly, "We weren't fighting bikers. We were fighting an army with lawyers and accountants." And yet, as brutal as it was, it worked. The Rock

Machine collapsed, patched over by the Bandidos, who themselves would implode in the infamous 2006 Shedden massacre. Boucher's war cleared the board. Quebec was his.

As the Rock Machine was being buried, the Hells Angels turned Quebec into a supply hub. Cocaine from Colombia, meth from the Midwest, pills from Europe, it all flowed through their channels. They didn't just deal drugs, they taxed them. Independent dealers paid tribute or got buried. Wholesale suppliers paid to play. They weren't just outlaws. They were organized. Ruthless. Professional. The Angels ran the streets like a multinational cartel in denim and chrome. They didn't rely on chaos. They built a system, a militarized, money-making machine where every cog had a purpose and every patch came with power.

This was no garage gang. It was a criminal syndicate with a corporate flowchart fueled by blow, muscle, and fear.

Let's meet them.

At the Top, the Nomads.

The Boardroom Killers. The Nomad chapter was the elite of the elite. No fixed turf. No boundaries. Just power. Based in Montreal, operating in shadows, they weren't bound by geography. They were bound by loyalty and purpose. These were Boucher's trusted few, the generals, the men who made war, struck alliances, and enforced order with precision.

They made the high-level decisions, who got taxed, who got green-lit for murder, which territories got absorbed, and who got tossed to the wolves. They weren't the guys riding loud through the suburbs. They were the ones signing death warrants in silence. When a hit needed approval, it came from the Nomads. When a major shipment landed at the Port of

Montreal, it was their pipeline. When someone betrayed the club, it was the Nomads who orchestrated the funeral. Their clubhouse on Bennett Street was their fortress, part gym, part war room, part throne room.

Below the Nomads, the Chartered Chapters.

The territorial arms of the organization. Each chapter, Quebec City, Sherbrooke, Trois-Rivières, and Halifax, ran its own turf like a franchise. They controlled distribution, enforced discipline, taxed independent dealers, and oversaw street-level operations. They kept the peace between puppet clubs. They made sure the money made it upstream. Think of them as regional managers responsible for performance, order, and revenue. If things got messy in their territory, if a shipment disappeared, if a dealer stopped paying tribute, they handled it fast and loud. Disrespect a full-patch member in their region? You didn't get a warning. You got a bullet.

The Support Clubs.

This was Boucher's masterstroke. They were ghost soldiers and human shields. Names like the Evil Ones, Death Riders, Rockers. To outsiders, they looked like wannabes, cheap jackets, off-brand patches. But to the Hells Angels, they were strategic assets, disposable soldiers in the war for control. These crews moved product, ran collections, handled hits, and absorbed the heat. When the cops came knocking, it wasn't the Nomads getting cuffed. It was some kid with a support patch, a rap sheet, and no lawyer. The Angels kept their hands clean while these guys took the charges, the bullets, the risks. They were meat shields with motors. And they were hungry to prove themselves.

If you did your job, maybe, just maybe, you'd one day get invited to hang around the mother chapter. Maybe earn that red-and-white patch. But most didn't make it that far. They bled for the patch. They died trying to earn it.

This layered structure wasn't just smart, it was bulletproof. Violence flowed downhill from Nomads to chapters, from chapters to support clubs, and finally to the streets. Money flowed uphill from crack corners to strip clubs to patch-holders to the Nomads' coffers.

If cops cracked a support club? Big deal. No trail to the top. No fingerprints. No voices on wiretaps. Cases collapsed. Charges didn't stick. The Angels stayed in the wind, running the streets without ever standing in them. It was a criminal pyramid with chrome handlebars and military discipline. That's why cops couldn't nail Boucher for years.

By the early 1990s, Mom Boucher wasn't just a biker anymore. He was a brand. Gone was the wild-eyed street brawler from Pointe-aux-Trembles, the skinhead bruiser who once prowled alleyways with the white supremacist SS crew. Boucher had evolved, refined his game, polished his image, and built a criminal enterprise that moved like a Fortune 500 company with blood on its ledger.

But make no mistake, the monster was still in there. He'd just put on a better suit. By the time he rose to lead the Hells Angels Nomads chapter, Boucher was a man transformed. The hard drugs, the late-night chaos, the barroom brawls, those were for grunts. Boucher played a higher game. He barely touched drugs, claiming to drink only alcohol and even that was in moderation. He was up early, always. Like clockwork, he met his lieutenants around 9:30 a.m. each morning, punctual as a CEO opening his war room.

But this wasn't just about health or discipline. It was strategy. Boucher understood the law. He knew surveillance was everywhere. Wiretaps, bugs, informants. So, he got clever. Whenever he needed to discuss something sensitive with his crew, he hired his lawyer to be present. That single move turned their biker sit-downs into legally protected meetings under attorney-client privilege. No wiretaps. No recordings. No admissible evidence. It was brilliant. And it worked.

Back home, Boucher lived nothing like the street thugs he commanded. He'd gone full Don, a kingpin in leather and gold. He bought himself a gated mansion in the south end of Montreal, complete with lush gardens, a long driveway, and horse stables out back. Not just for show. Horses were a passion. And nothing screamed power like riding a quarter horse across your own land, a cigar in one hand and a Glock tucked in your waistband.

But his empire didn't stop at Quebec. Mom had real estate in Acapulco, Mexico, beachfront properties, and hilltop villas registered under shell companies. There, he played the part of international developer, hosting lavish parties for senior officers of the Acapulco police, one of the most crooked forces in the Western Hemisphere. Booze flowed, envelopes were passed, and alliances were built far from the eyes of Canadian law enforcement.

Why Mexico? Simple. He couldn't enter the United States. His rap sheet was too long, too bloody. America didn't want him. So, he built his offshore kingdom where the law was cheap and the beaches were warm.

When Boucher filed his Canadian income taxes, and he did, carefully, he never listed "Biker Boss" as his job. Instead, he rotated identities like a man changing masks. Chef, construction worker, used car dealer, real estate investor. It was a smokescreen thick enough to throw off the scent, at least for a while. The image he crafted was that of a rugged entrepreneur, rough around the edges but legitimate enough to make audits annoying and court cases slippery. But everyone who mattered knew the truth. He was the architect of *Les Hells'* empire in Quebec, a man who ruled through fear, respect, and ruthless business acumen.

While Quebec bled, the Hells Angels expanded west. Ontario, Alberta, B.C., and the Maritimes weren't just territories. They were prizes. Ontario's outlaw scene had been fragmented. With the Angels' playbook of coercion, diplomacy, and spectacle, they absorbed or eliminated clubs like the Para-Dice Riders and Loners. Resistance was met with firebombs or offers no one refused.

Boucher may have waged war, but Walter "Nurget" Stadnick, Canada's national president, built the empire.

Stadnick wasn't flashy. He was strategic. Born in Hamilton, he understood that if the Angels wanted national supremacy, they couldn't be seen as a Quebec gang. Under his guidance, they created a true coast-to-coast network. Every new chapter had to be approved, trained, and brought in line.

In British Columbia, the biker scene was already heavy with organized crime. Asian triads, Indo-Canadian drug crews, and independent operators. But the Angels played long ball. They patched over the Satan's Angels and took the Lower Mainland inch by inch, building alliances instead of just bloodshed.

By the late 1990s, there were more Hells Angels chapters in Canada than anywhere outside the United States. They weren't just bikers. They were landlords, smugglers, taxmen, and enforcers. They had judges, customs officers, and construction bosses on their payrolls.

But Boucher thought he was untouchable. He wasn't just a man with a patch. He was a general. A tactician. A ghost with a smirk. Mom Boucher, once a prison punk with a rape conviction, had risen through the blood-soaked streets of Montreal to become the most feared outlaw in the province. The streets whispered his name. Police watched from the shadows. The justice system, he believed, was a rigged game. So, he did what men like him do. He set the table on fire.

By 1997, his grip on Quebec's drug trade was ironclad. His reach extended from back alleys to luxury condos to Acapulco resorts. But in the back of his mind, one thing kept gnawing at him. There was a *Délateur*. A rat. Word had leaked from within RCMP intelligence. Someone inside the Angels was talking. And if there was anything Boucher hated more than losing power, it was betrayal.

So, he began hunting.

The turning point came in March 1997. Aimé Simard, a cold-blooded killer for the Rockers, a Hells Angels puppet crew, broke the code. He flipped. Faced with the wall of federal time and likely dead the minute he got out, Simard cut a deal. Boucher exploded. This wasn't the first betrayal. Yves "Apache" Trudeau had already turned on the Angels in the '80s, confessing to 43 murders in exchange for a sweetheart deal. Then Serge Quesnel flipped in the early '90s.

Three hitmen, all linked to the Angels. Three deals with the Crown. It was a pattern Boucher could no longer ignore.

In his twisted logic, the only way to stop the leaks was to poison the well. Make it too dangerous for the justice system to do deals at all. Terrorize them. Frighten the Crown. Kill the messengers. It wasn't about profit anymore. It was about the message. And the message was war. In Boucher's eyes, Quebec's justice system wasn't sacred. It was an enemy institution. He called the shots, but judges, prosecutors, and prison guards were the gatekeepers to power. And they were getting too bold. Boucher zeroed in on what he considered the system's weak link. Prison guards. Blue-collar, unarmed, and unsuspecting. They were the lowest rung and the perfect targets.

He chose two Nomads prospects. Stéphane "Godasse" Gagné, a wiry, jittery thug with a need to prove himself, and André "Toots" Tousignant, a man with dead eyes and a loose leash. Boucher gave the order. No names. No warnings. Just bullets.

June 26, 1997. Dianne Lavigne had just finished her shift at Bordeaux prison. It was late. She was driving home along a quiet stretch of road in her silver Toyota. She never saw them coming. A motorcycle pulled up alongside her.

Pop. Pop. Pop.

Three shots through the window. Lavigne died before the car drifted to a stop. She was 42. A mother. A civil servant. A target of war. When Gagné later met Boucher to debrief, he told him the truth. "I killed a woman." Boucher didn't flinch. He didn't blink. "That's good, Godasse. It doesn't matter that she had tits." That line would come back to haunt him. But not yet.

September 8, 1997. The sun hadn't fully risen when prison guard Pierre Rondeau started his shift, manning a prison transport van with his partner, Robert Corriveau. At 8:40 a.m., as they pulled away from the Rivière-des-Prairies detention center, a black car appeared in their rearview.

Then, gunfire.

The windshield exploded. Rondeau took two rounds to the head and died instantly. Corriveau was wounded but survived, the side of his face shredded by shrapnel. The van crashed into a pole near Pie-IX Boulevard. The city stopped cold. Civilians screamed. Cops were stunned. No one is safe.

The killings weren't just murder. They were psychological warfare. Judges requested police escorts. Prosecutors worked behind bulletproof glass. Guards refused overtime. Morale plummeted. The media spun it like a biker blitzkrieg. The public, for all its horror, couldn't look away. And Boucher, calm, cocky, and calculating, was about to become more than just a suspect. He was about to become a legend.

December 18, 1997. Boucher was arrested and charged with ordering the murders of Lavigne and Rondeau. Two counts of first-degree murder. Quebec braced itself for a reckoning. But it didn't get one. The trial was a circus. Witnesses were terrified. Evidence was flimsy. The aura of invincibility surrounded Boucher like smoke. He was acquitted. And the reaction? Applause. Boucher was carried out of the courtroom on the shoulders of his brothers. Cameras flashed. Reporters snapped quotes. In the eyes of some, he wasn't a killer. He was a symbol of defiance. An outlaw prince who had beaten the system.

Weeks later, Boucher swaggered into the Molson Centre in Montreal to watch the middleweight bout between David Hilton and Stéphane Ouellet. As he took his seat, the crowd stood and cheered. Hundreds lined up for autographs. Grown men patted him on the back. Women blew kisses. One tabloid called him *"the people's gangster."* In a province disillusioned with politics and power, Boucher had become something, a folk hero.

Twisted, yeah, but that's how it was.

He would ride his Harley through Hochelaga-Maisonneuve, his gang flanking him like royalty. Locals leaned out of balconies, clapping. Kids waved. Some even saluted. To the working class, he was one of them. To the media, he was a story that sold. And to the underworld, he was the standard.

But to the police, he was unfinished business. Because behind the folklore, the murder charges, and the smirks, there was still blood on the pavement. And too many names on the list.

So, here's the picture by the end of the '90s. Two empires were humming like freight trains on parallel tracks, both quiet, both rich, both ruthless. The Rizzutos ran the construction sites, unions, and political backrooms. The Angels ran the highways, street corners, and drug dens. Different styles, same goal. Control. And when their worlds overlapped, the Mafia running the docks, the Angels ruling the streets, they made a deal. Business over blood.

For a while, it worked. But in the underworld? Truces are just loaded guns sitting on the table. Sooner or later, somebody pulls the trigger.

# Chapter 3

# The Fragile Alliance

Montreal wasn't alive, it was throbbing, restless, hungry. That place had a pulse, and it wasn't coming from jazz bars or cathedral bells. No. It was the sound of envelopes sliding across tables, car doors slamming before somebody disappeared, the dull boom of a bomb echoing through the night. You had the polite Montreal everyone knew, baguettes, bagels, and bilingual manners. And then you had the Montreal that mattered. The one under the floorboards. The one that paid.

By the 1990s, the place was a contradiction in a leather jacket. Catholic yet carnal, sophisticated yet savage, Old World manners chasing New World money. Perfect ground for organized crime. And if you wanted to understand it? You had to start at the water.

The St. Lawrence wasn't just geography. It was the artery of Canada. Everything flowed through it. Wheat, oil, steel... and tons of dope. Cocaine, hash, heroin, you name it, it all slipped past customs, stacked inside those endless cargo containers. A million of 'em a year at the Port of Montreal. Most were legit. But a few? A few were packed tighter than Christmas stockings with enough powder to light up a province.

The port was a colossus. Cranes swinging like iron monsters, forklifts buzzing like angry bees, containers stacked so high they blotted out the skyline. A box labeled "ceramic tiles" might actually be carrying 300 kilos of coke. "Machine parts"? Maybe barrels of hash oil from Pakistan. "Frozen fish"? Yeah, with bricks of Colombian flake nestled in the ice. To regular people, it looked like international commerce. To the people who mattered, it was a candy store. The port was the crown jewel.

In the old days, Nicolo greased it with handshakes and charm, bribing customs like it was an Italian art. His kid, Vito? He turned it into a masterpiece. The man ran the port like it was his living room. Inspectors suddenly went blind. Union bosses suddenly remembered their cousins needed jobs. Cameras conveniently broke. Forklifts diverted containers by "accident."

Every crack in the system was another opening for the Rizzutos. And they didn't just pay people. They seduced them. A wedding invite for one guy. An envelope for another. A problem fixed, a cousin promoted, a mortgage paid off. Everyone got a taste. Everyone looked the other way.

That's how Montreal became the North American gateway for the Sicilian pipeline. Coke from Medellín. Heroin from the Golden Crescent. Hash from the Middle East. It all came through, quiet as a ghost, and slipped inland before the cops even knew it was there.

It all started with cocaine. It always does.

Here's the thing. Moving drugs in is one thing. Getting them out? That's another. And that's where the Hells Angels came roaring in.

The Angels weren't diplomats. They didn't smile and hand you a glass of wine like Vito. They didn't charm inspectors. They just scared the shit out of everyone. Their language wasn't Sicilian dialect. It was the roar of Harleys, the smell of leather and bourbon, and fists that didn't ask twice.

By the late '90s, under Mom Boucher, they weren't a gang anymore. They were an army. Quebec was theirs. They had puppet clubs in every corner, guys willing to bleed for a chance at that death-head patch. They owned the highways. If coke was leaving Montreal, it was strapped inside a refrigerated truck, hidden in a coffin inside a funeral van, or shoved under the floorboards of a semi hauling pork bellies. And always, always, under Angel protection.

Nobody moved product in Quebec without their blessing. You tried, you got a warning, maybe your bike got torched. Push your luck, you caught a bullet. Simple as that.

And Mom wasn't just a cartoon thug with tattoos. He was a micromanaging psychopath with ambitions the size of the Jacques Cartier Bridge. "Mom" because he hovered over every detail. Guys said he'd show up with a checklist like some PTA mother. "You got your guns? You mapped your exit? You packed lunch?" He didn't just want jobs done. He wanted them done his way. And his way was ruthless.

And he didn't want to sling dime bags on street corners. He wanted containers. Crates. Cargo by the ton. He didn't want to be a biker boss. He wanted to be a kingpin. He studied the Mafia like it was a textbook. The suits, the laundering, the way they bought silence instead of wasting bullets. He wanted that, but louder, scarier. He wanted to show the old men in silk shirts that the boys in denim and leather could run the show too.

And that's how it happened. The uneasy truce.

See, the Rizzutos had the port. The Angels had the streets. One couldn't work without the other. So, they did business. No contracts, no champagne toasts. Just quiet sit-downs in strip club back rooms, or private rooms in steak joints where the waiters didn't speak English and the doors locked from the inside.

The deal was simple. The Mafia imported. The Angels distributed. Bulk coke came in through containers stamped "bananas" or "auto parts." Mob trucks picked it up and moved it to warehouses. Then the bikers took over. They chopped it, cut it, bagged it, and moved it through the pipeline, Halifax to Vancouver, Buffalo to Boston. Every street dealer, every nightclub pusher, every indie hustler kicked up. The Rizzutos took their cut. The Angels took theirs.

And the money? It poured in like oil.

The cash came in faster than anyone could count. Dirty, sweaty cash stuffed in duffel bags. Tens of millions. But you can't just dump duffels into a bank. You need books that sing. So, they made the books sing.

One week, it's a strip club. Books show record nights on paper, fifty grand in "lap dances." Please. Nobody's getting that many dances. That was coke money, washed and deposited as "entertainment revenue."

Next week, it's a construction company. They win a bid to pour concrete for a city project, double the competitor's price. But nobody says a word, because inspectors are already on the take. They were pulling down government contracts and washed cartel money with the same pour of concrete.

Real estate was the jewel. Condos in Laval were just laundromats with better views. Office towers downtown. Bought in cash, flipped, resold. Real estate in Laval went through the roof. Everybody ate. By the time Revenue Canada took a look, it was clean as a whistle. And the bikers learned fast. You don't flash stacks. You buy property. You buy respect. You buy insulation.

But let's be clear, they weren't friends. Not even close.

The Mafia saw the Angels as wild animals. Loud. Uncouth. No class. The Angels saw the Mafia as prissy, silk-shirt clowns too scared to get their hands dirty. But they both saw the money. And money? In this world, it comes before pride.

Best way to explain it? Montreal was a chessboard.

Vito was the chess master. Quiet, patient, always three moves ahead. Polished suits, three languages, never raising his voice, like velvet over a straight razor. He could settle a million-dollar dispute with a handshake and a smile that said, "Push me, and you vanish."

Boucher? He was the wrecking ball. He didn't play chess. He kicked the board over and shot the other guy in the face. Built in prison, fueled by rage, a tactician with ice water in his veins. He didn't do handshakes. He did ultimatums. You crossed him. You didn't get a warning. You got two Rockers with Tec-9s showing up at your bar, spraying the place till the walls bled.

That's the thing. They needed each other. They respected each other. But respect here? It's just another word for not today.

And the city? The city adjusted. Grannies in Little Italy kissed Vito's hand outside Sunday mass. Kids in Hochelaga waved at Boucher as he roared by on his Harley. Politicians smiled for photo ops while their campaign envelopes were stuffed with cash.

It was balance. Fragile. But balance.

On the docks, a customs agent whistled as he waved through a container, knowing damn well it smelled like Colombian snow. On Autoroute 20, a trucker hauling pork bellies carried an extra 500 kilos of coke under a false floor, riding with a biker escort in the next lane. In Little Italy, Vito sipped espresso outside a café, kissed babies, shook hands, and looked like a neighborhood saint. Across town, Boucher was bench pressing at Pro-Gym, planning his next move in sweat and steel.

It was two empires. One in silk, one in leather. Sharing the city like divorced parents splitting custody of a kid. Montreal belonged to both.

But here's the thing about alliances in the underworld. They don't last. They're like loaded guns. Useful, but always dangerous. One day, someone pulls the trigger. And when that day came, Montreal didn't hum anymore. It screamed.

Now, people outside thought it was all random. Another car bomb. Another body in an alley. Another funeral with Cadillacs parked three deep outside a church. To the newspapers, it was chaos. To the people in the life? It was order.

See, none of it was random. A guy didn't just disappear because he owed twenty bucks. He disappeared because he missed a tax payment three times. Or because he disrespected the wrong man in front of the wrong eyes. Violence was management. It was accounting with bullets. The Mafia handled balance with sit-downs, arbitration, a little old-country theater. The bikers handled it with a fist or a chain. But the goal was the same. Keep the wheels turning, keep the money flowing. And somehow, for almost a decade, it worked.

Picture this. The back room of a Laval strip club. Red velvet couches, mirrors on the wall, cigarette smoke hanging like a curtain. On one side, Vito's *consigliere*, maybe Paolo Renda, suit pressed, shoes polished. On the other, a biker captain, shaved head, leather cut tossed over a chair.

The talk? All business.

"You lost two keys last week."

"Not lost. Stolen. Your problem, not ours."

"We'll find the thief. But you eat half the loss."

"Fuck that."

Silence. Eyes narrow. Then Renda smiles, sips his espresso, and says, "Half… or nobody eats."

That's diplomacy, Mafia-style. A threat wrapped in velvet. Most times, it worked. When it didn't, well… that's when the Rockers got called in, and somebody's name got scratched off the ledger.

Boucher, for his part, wasn't building a street crew. He was building infrastructure. Couriers on backroads and bus terminals. Dispatchers with burners and codes. Cold storage where white powder slept beside pork. Mechanics, customs brokers, grease men who made seizures vanish and doors stay shut. The real protection wasn't Kevlar. It was courtrooms and customs booths. The Mafia had learned that long ago, judges who misplaced warrants, border agents who waved through funny manifests, cops who leaked raid dates. Boucher wanted all of it. Not just fear on the street, but insulation in the system.

It worked because both sides evolved. In rare cases, bikers even slid into "associate" slots inside the Rizzuto Family, unthinkable a decade earlier. Bloodlines mattered less than bottom lines. Deliver and you ate. Money was the engine.

But nothing this big lasts. Stack enough money, enough bodies, enough secrets, and cracks start showing.

The cops weren't geniuses, but they weren't blind. RCMP surveillance was tightening. Wiretaps buzzed on payphones. Informants whispered. Every time a biker got nailed with a trunk full of dope, there was a chance he'd flip. Every time a Mafia soldier got caught skimming, there was a chance he'd rat. The Angels knew it. Yves "Apache" Trudeau flipped in the '80s, confessed to over forty murders. Then Aimé Simard in '97. Rats in the walls.

Boucher's solution? Kill the system itself. Judges, prosecutors, prison guards. Suddenly, they were targets. Madness, sure. But for a while, it worked. Fear shuts mouths faster than money.

Vito? He hated chaos. He knew blood in the streets brought heat. But he tolerated it, because for him, silence was worth the mess.

And although wolves and lions can drink from the same river, they'll never hunt together. Deep down, both sides knew it. Vito wanted invisibility, respect, diplomacy, legacy. Boucher wanted domination, fear, control, his name in lights. Those two visions don't mix. Oil and holy water. Not forever.

And so, Montreal kept humming, thumping, bleeding. For a time, it was business over blood. But in this world? Business always leads to blood.

Everybody got rich. Everybody got comfortable. That's when people stop watching their backs. Politicians bragged about construction booms while pocketing envelopes. Judges laughed over wine poured by the men they were supposed to convict. Biker bosses strutted like rock stars. Mafia dons toasted with champagne.

But behind the curtains, the walls were shaking. The Americans flipped Joseph Massino, boss of the Bonannos. Suddenly, Vito's role in that 1981 triple murder in New York was back on the table. Extradition papers started moving. The "Teflon Don of Canada" had cracks in his armor.

And *Les Hells*? The Quebec Biker War had burned too hot, too long. Too many bodies. Too many innocents caught in crossfire. Public opinion turned. The cops smelled blood. Operation SharQc. Operation Springtime. Operation Magot. Operation Mastiff. They were coming.

The empire that looked bulletproof was about to be tested.

So yeah, in the '90s, Montreal was a city run by two monarchies. One in silk suits. One in leather cuts. They coexisted because they had to. They shared the throne because the money demanded it.

But don't kid yourself. They weren't brothers. They were predators circling the same carcass, careful not to bite each other too soon.

And like every predator, eventually hunger wins.

Business came first. But blood? Blood waited in the hallway. And when the door finally opened, business stepped out, and blood stepped in.

# Part II: The Brotherhood

## Chapter 4

## Business Over Blood

By the early 1990s, the old rules were gone. Forget all that honor and family bullshit. Respect didn't mean kissing rings anymore. It meant product, power, and profit. This wasn't your grandfather's Mafia, sitting around with rosaries and red wine. It wasn't a bunch of fringe bikers chasing bar fights and tail lights. No, this was the new era. This was suits and leather jackets shaking hands, running a criminal economy that pumped drugs, guns, and blood money through the veins of Canada like it was Wall Street with silencers.

The Rizzutos and Angels were never built to get along. One came from Sicily, a world of whispers and *omertà*, saints on the walls and knives in the dark. The other roared up out of California like an oil-stained demon, blasting down highways on Harleys, snarling, loud, always ready to swing first and ask questions never. But in Montreal, they saw each other for what they really were, not enemies, not rivals, but assets. And in this city of frozen rivers and hot money, they built something monstrous together.

See, Montreal was a gold mine of dope pipelines. Coke from Medellín, hash bricks from Morocco, AKs from Detroit, all of it moving through a criminal economy. The Rizzutos had the keys to the port. The Angels had the keys to the streets. It was like a lock clicking open. Perfect fit if you ignored the blood.

Now, Vito wasn't some street-corner punk with a *stiletto* in his boot. The guy was running a symphony while the rest banged on pots and pans. He could sit down with Colombians, Calabrians, New York bosses, Sicilians back home, and somehow, everyone walked out thinking they won. He didn't scream. He didn't threaten. He smiled, he charmed, he got what he wanted. Vito didn't pull triggers. He pulled strings. And one of those strings led straight to the Hells Angels.

Then, you had Mom Boucher. This guy wasn't about subtlety. He was about dominance. He ruled Quebec's biker scene with raw force, clubhouses turned into bunkers, daylight hits on rivals, steel-toe boots stomping out competition. If Vito was the CEO, Boucher was the warlord. And if the two of them could make peace, even for a while, well, the whole city would bend under it.

What started out as cautious cooperation, coke for control, quickly turned into a full-fledged empire. The Mafia handled importation. The Angels handled transportation, territory, and muscle. And the cash? It never stopped moving.

Now, here's the genius of it. They didn't just deal dope. They learned how to wash it. Montreal had always been greasy with cash, but these two turned the whole economy into a laundromat. A kilo of coke paid for somebody's mortgage. Blood money built condos in Laval. Nightclubs ran on laundered bills. Strip joints weren't just about tits and neon. They were cash funnels, business hubs. Dirty bills went in, crisp profits came out.

The Rizzutos had the playbook. Vito spent years building front companies that looked cleaner than the Pope's sheets. Concrete firms, excavation crews, real estate companies, all legal on paper, all rotten at the core. Public contracts got rigged, inspectors paid off, zoning boards leaned the right way. Nobody blinked when a mob-connected concrete firm suddenly posted record profits. Looked like business. Smelled like success. It was pure filth.

The bikers weren't so slick at first. Their money moved through tattoo parlors, strip clubs, auto shops, cash in, cash out, no finesse. But Mom wasn't dumb. He saw what the Sicilians were doing. Offshore accounts. Fake invoices. Paper trails that led nowhere. The Angels started copying it. A Harley shop in Laval might invoice eighty grand for "custom parts." No parts ever showed. Just a few bricks got moved, and payments settled.

Pretty soon, they were even teaming up on businesses and began co-investing in vice operations. Nightclubs across Montreal, some upscale, others underground, became joint ventures. Bikers ran security. Mobsters ran the books. Drug sales were managed at arm's length through intermediaries, and cash got funneled through liquor sales, event promotions, and silent partners in real estate. If you wanted to party in Montreal in the '90s, chances are you were dancing on a floor paid for with blood money.

In Vancouver and Toronto, the model was replicated. Rizzuto-affiliated money funded condo developments and car dealerships. Biker-backed enforcers protected distribution hubs. In Calgary and Edmonton, real estate and construction laundering bloomed. What emerged was a decentralized but interconnected empire. Like a web spun in smoke and grease, stretching across the country, hiding in plain sight. At the heart of it all was mutual respect, not affection.

The Rizzutos saw the Angels as useful. Dangerous, yes. Unpredictable at times. But disciplined, organized, and loyal to their own. They weren't junkies or thugs. They were military. The Angels, for their part, saw the Rizzutos as necessary. The Mafia brought product, protection, and most importantly, legitimacy. Affiliation with the Rizzutos elevated the Angels beyond the outlaw stereotype. It meant they weren't just street-level hoodlums. They were partners in a billion-dollar criminal infrastructure. But it was always respect born of calculation, not trust. Each side watched the other carefully. When a joint nightclub took in more than expected, both sides counted the money separately. When a new shipment came through the port, both sent their own men to "supervise."

Still, for nearly a decade, it worked. And the money flowed. There were no oaths. No blood rituals. No saints watching over their deals. The Rizzutos and Angels didn't need ceremony. They had an understanding. Their alliance wasn't about brotherhood. It was about business. And business needed order. This was the silent covenant of the Canadian underworld built not on loyalty, but calculation. Two empires, speaking in different dialects of violence, came to a truce not because they trusted each other, but because they feared what chaos would cost. In that fear, they forged rules. Not written down but understood with deadly clarity.

They called it respect. What it really was... was survival.

And the meetings that made it all work? Forget about Hollywood drama. No fireplaces, no blood oaths, no dramatic music. Just silence, tension, espresso, and stale smoke. Neutral ground. An Italian café in Saint-Léonard. A biker strip joint in Laval. A chalet up in the Laurentians. Windowless garages in Longueuil. These were the "embassies" of the Brotherhood, neutral ground where empire-makers sat down to keep blood off the streets.

Before every sit-down, the place got swept. Not by captains, but by nobodies, prospects, hang-arounds, errand boys. Guys with no heat and no warrants. They'd sit at the bar, scan the exits, check for narcs. Only when the coast was clear did the real players show.

Rizzuto guys like *consigliere* Paolo Renda or *capo* Francesco Arcadi showed up in slick suits, pressed slacks, soft shoes. Angels guys like Mom's right-hand men, David "Wolf" Carroll or Normand Robitaille, arrived with shaved heads, leather cuts, heavy boots. Different tribes, same rules. No guns on the table, no flexing, no phones. These were the diplomats of darkness. They negotiated drug disputes, renegotiated revenue splits, and de-escalated beefs before they turned into bloodbaths. They didn't just carry messages. They interpreted meaning.

The talks were polite but colder than ice. Like high-level business negotiations dipped in menace. A missed shipment? A tax dispute on meth profits? A dead associate found in a ditch near Repentigny? It all got discussed over espresso or scotch, in tones calm enough to be eerie, like accountants reviewing quarterly numbers. Voices low, faces blank. If a beef couldn't be handled right there, it went up the ladder. And if it got to Vito or Boucher, the solution was final. No appeals.

That was the covenant. Not brotherhood, business. Business needed order, and order meant rules. Everybody played by them, or else.

But rules are only as strong as the men who enforce them. And in the dark corridors of the Rizzuto-Angels alliance, enforcement wasn't just about punishment. It was about messaging. A missed payment. A loose mouth. A disrespectful nod at the wrong man. These weren't petty missteps. They were sparks in a room full of gas. Someone had to keep the peace. And someone had to remind everyone what happened when you broke it.

Enter the enforcers. Messengers with brass knuckles that kept the system intact. And when they didn't, when a rogue outsider set up shop without permission, retaliation came fast.

See, there was a hierarchy to enforcement.

First Offense. A message delivered face-to-face or through a lieutenant. Usually calm. Often delivered in public, to remind the offender they were being watched.

Second Offense. Physical enforcement. A visit with a ball-peen hammer. A vandalized car. A raid on a stash house. Sometimes done personally, sometimes subcontracted to street-level enforcers, guys owed favors or looking to earn stripes.

Third Offense. Termination. A news report about an unidentified body found in the Saint Lawrence River. Quiet or loud, depending on the optics. The Angels preferred spectacular. The Mafia preferred to be invisible. But the result was the same. His name wasn't crossed out on the roster. It was buried.

Disrespect during a sit-down? That was treated as a second or third offense immediately, depending on who you insulted. There were no untouchables. Even within their own crews, the code was enforced without mercy. An Angel who disrespected a patched brother was given the "clubhouse justice," a brutal in-house beating that could leave a man crippled or stripped of his patch. A Mafia associate who mishandled product or lied to a superior? Gone. One day, he was at a café on Jean-Talon, the next, his mother was filing a missing person's report while the cops looked the other way.

This mutual brutality created trust, not emotional trust, but operational trust. Both sides knew the other could handle discipline internally. That meant fewer wars. Fewer headlines. And more profit.

But not every rule-breaker needed to be buried. Sometimes, they just needed to be reminded. The Mob's enforcement style was cold and surgical. Vito didn't like noise. His ideal outcome? The problem disappears, and no one ever hears about it. A missed drug tax? A quiet sit-down with a warning. Maybe your car explodes at 3 a.m. No bodies. Just messages.

If a biker had beef with a mob guy, he didn't handle it solo. He told his sergeant-at-arms. He told an intermediary. The intermediary set up a sit-down with the Rizzuto's contact. Violence skipped a generation of men unless it was authorized at the top.

Same for the other side. If a Rizzuto associate got ripped off by a low-level Angel, the word went up the ladder. If the biker leadership agreed it was a breach, they'd fix it. Quietly. Sometimes with money. Sometimes with a closed casket. This wasn't out of kindness. It was risk management. Both crews knew the damage one hot-headed soldier could cause. A shooting at the wrong time, in the wrong borough, could undo months of profit and trigger the kind of law enforcement heat neither side wanted.

So, they built a culture of cold discipline.

Vito kept *omertà* with a soft touch until the day it had to tighten like a noose. His men didn't rant in public. They didn't wave guns in clubs. They moved like shadows. Orders were passed down through lookouts, waiters, and janitors who owed favors.

The bikers played it differently. No disrespect to a full-patch member went unanswered. No patch worn in the presence of the Mafia unless cleared. Clubhouses were sacred. And when it came to punishment, they were as brutal as they were theatrical. A dealer caught skimming would be stripped, beaten, and dumped in a riverbank ditch naked and leaking blood. They didn't just punish. They performed. But both styles served the same purpose. To keep the wheels of business turning.

Beatings, burnings, or sudden disappearances. But when it came to the Rizzutos, even the most violent Angels dialed it back. They knew what Vito represented. He was a man who could have you buried in a vineyard in Sicily before your brothers even knew you were gone.

Sometimes, the most powerful men in the room didn't say much. They didn't need to. That's what translators were for, not of language, but of subculture. Raynald Desjardins was the best of them. A French-Canadian with Mafia ties and biker respect, he was the rare figure fluent in both dialects of crime. He could walk into a café with a Rizzuto *consigliere*, then cross the street to a biker garage and speak their language. Money, respect, risk, revenge.

A Rizzuto underboss might say, "He disrespected the table." The intermediary knew that didn't mean hurt feelings. It meant territory had been violated. They explained why a delayed shipment wasn't a double-cross, or why a missing envelope wasn't a reason to put a bullet behind someone's ear. And there needed to be restitution or retaliation. In biker code, "That guy's running hot" might mean a prospect was bragging about deals that should've stayed silent. Intermediaries translated that into Mafia terms. Security risk, potential liability, green light for correction.

Without them, the alliance wouldn't have lasted a year. At its peak, the code worked. Not because it was sacred. But because it was smart. The port kept humming. The drugs kept flowing. The police were two steps behind. And the city underneath the jazz bars, the concrete, the snow was ruled by men who spoke in nods and moved billions without moving their mouths.

But everyone knew the truth. Codes only hold as long as everyone plays by them. And beneath the surface, some had already started cheating. Every empire draws borders. The underworld is no different. And while the lines that divided the Rizzuto Family and the Hells Angels weren't etched on any map, everyone knew exactly where they ran and what happened when you crossed them.

This was criminal cartography. Montreal was the heart, Quebec the spine, and Canada the body they aimed to control. But territory wasn't just geography. It was economy. It was reputation. And it was war if the wrong guy set foot on the wrong block. To maintain the alliance, they had to share the country. So, they sliced it like a pie, each piece carved with blood and strategy.

Look, the city was sacred. Montreal belonged to the Rizzutos. They owned the port. That meant they owned the gateway where the coke came in, the hash got unboxed, and the chemicals for biker meth were offloaded under customs agents' noses. The Rizzutos controlled the political grease. The zoning boards, the city inspectors, the low-level cops who knew when to look the other way. Their front businesses were everywhere. Concrete companies, nightclubs, strip bars, cigar lounges. The whole operation ran on quiet intimidation and invisible hands.

The Angels didn't contest it. They didn't need to. They had the streets. The biker chapters owned street-level distribution in East End Montreal, Laval, and down into Longueuil. Meth labs ran in rural barns. Dealerships operated in tattoo parlors, biker bars, and garages disguised as auto shops. They taxed independent dealers, ran protection rackets, and delivered fear with terrifying efficiency. If you bought blow on St Denis Street or E on a dance floor in Laval, odds are it passed through both hands. Mafia-imported, biker-distributed. The handshake at the top became a vice grip at the street level.

Beyond Montreal, Quebec was checkerboarded with influence. The Angels spread like a spiked virus. Clubhouses popped up in Sherbrooke, Trois-Rivières, Val-d'Or. Puppet clubs, loosely affiliated biker gangs who kicked up profits, filled in the gaps, giving the Angels total coverage from small towns to highways. This made them invaluable to the

Rizzutos. No matter how good your cocaine supply was, it didn't move itself. The bikers were the arteries.

Meanwhile, the Mafia's reach spread through construction bids and property schemes. From Ottawa to the Saguenay, they brokered contracts, bought politicians, and buried their money under legitimate blueprints.

The two worlds overlapped most in laundering operations. A Mafia-owned construction company might hire a biker-run security team. A biker strip club in Gatineau might get "investment" from a Rizzuto associate. These weren't accidental alliances. They were tactical mergers. Nothing tested the alliance more than profit.

To avoid bloodshed, they built an internal economy. A kilo brought in from Venezuela? That was a Mafia import. If the Angels moved it through their channels, the split might be 60/40 in favor of the Rizzutos. But if the product was cooked in a Quebec lab or moved through biker channels in Ontario or the West, the Angels might get the lion's share, or at least parity. Territory dictated tax. If a biker dealer operated in Rizzuto-controlled turf, he paid tribute, 10 to 30 percent, depending on the commodity. Same went for Mafia-affiliated dealers in biker-run regions. Violation wasn't met with lawsuits. It was met with shattered kneecaps or permanent disappearances.

Territory deals were often reviewed monthly. Sit-downs recalibrated profit percentages based on shifting market trends. If the Sinaloa pipeline dried up or a police bust interrupted a port route, the next shipment might require renegotiation. Nothing was permanent. Everything was provisional. This paranoia wasn't a flaw. It was the system's backbone. Because both sides knew, if the balance tipped too far, if one side got too rich, too loud, or too greedy, the alliance would collapse.

By the late '90s, the breaking point wasn't a question. It was a countdown.

# Chapter 5

# The Golden Years

Montreal, 1997. The city thrummed with power you didn't see but you sure as hell felt. Neon spilled across wet pavement, jazz curled out of basement clubs, and in the shadows, something rare was happening. For once, the underworld wasn't bleeding. It was thriving.

This was no longer a fragile pact held together by fear and profits. The Rizzutos and the Hells Angels had evolved into something bigger, something colder. An empire. A billion-dollar-a-year criminal machine powered by cocaine, corruption, and mutual need. That's not drug money. That's war budget money.

The Rizzutos and Angels were no longer just bosses of Montreal's back alleys. They were architects of a global syndicate, one that stretched from the jungles of Colombia to the ports of Croatia, from tattoo parlors in Vancouver to safehouses in Costa Rica. They weren't playing the local game. They were playing the world. And at the heart of it all was the cocaine pipeline. Powder white, pure, and soaked in blood.

Money moves mountains. Influence keeps them standing. The Rizzutos and the Angels didn't just move product. They moved systems. They didn't dodge law enforcement. They compromised it. They didn't just shake down unions. They embedded themselves within them. They weren't criminals hiding in shadows anymore. They were shareholders in the machinery of the state.

This wasn't just organized crime anymore. It was organized control. The violence didn't disappear. It got subcontracted. Hits were surgical, clean, and scarce. The streets stayed quiet, but only because the bosses demanded silence.

Vito had turned the Mafia into a multinational logistics empire. No longer just a crime family, it was a conglomerate of front companies, crooked unions, and political reach. He wore high-end Brioni suits, sipped espresso, and kept cops guessing with that smile that never gave anything away. Mom Boucher, who once ran Quebec like a paramilitary zone, was now focused on stability. Violence scared money. Stability printed it. Business was booming.

Together, they ran Canada's black market like CEOs in leather and silk. The mobster in the suit, the outlaw in the vest, two kings at the same table, running an empire from the shadows.

The Alliance governed a hidden country beneath the surface of Canada, complete with borders, departments, and enforcement agencies. A narco-state in all but name. It was mapped like a corporation. Every region had its role. Every city had a handler. Every street dealer was a cog in a billion-dollar engine.

The division of labor was surgical.

The Rizzutos ran the whole goddamn pipeline. The ports. The political grease. Vito's crew weren't street thugs. They were the brokers, the bankers, the strategists moving dope across continents.

Cocaine shipments moved from the jungles of Colombia to the docks of Montreal with less interference than a holiday postal package. Port customs were riddled with "helpers," dock supervisors, security guards, forklift operators. Some were paid. Some were family. Local cops in biker-heavy neighborhoods like Saint-Jérôme or Longueuil turned a blind eye. A few crossed lines completely, doing favors for money because they knew what would happen if they didn't.

Port employees were paid off in brown envelopes. Customs officers were told where to look and, more importantly, where not to. The Rizzuto machine had protection everywhere. Import/export companies in Lachine, numbered bank accounts in the Caymans, and lawyers on retainer who carried secrets heavier than briefcases. They had union reps in their pocket, city inspectors in their debt, and politicians whose campaigns ran on underworld donations.

From the Port of Montreal, cocaine arrived in containers labeled as coffee beans, textiles, or construction materials. Nobody blinked. By the time the paperwork cleared customs, thanks to paid-off agents or misfiled paperwork, it was already broken down, reboxed, and sent off in trucks wearing the paint jobs of legit construction outfits. Warehouses in Laval and Lachine stacked bricks like drywall.

Sometimes the loads took the scenic route. Hidden in banana crates, coffee shipments, furniture containers. Italian ports like Gioia Tauro and Palermo, where Sicilian allies helped move product through Mediterranean channels. Balkan ports where Albanians greased customs. Spanish docks, crooked inspectors, containers slipping past like ghosts. Coke left South America, touched Europe, and crossed the Atlantic scrubbed clean. The detour made it harder to trace and easier to manipulate.

But when cocaine made headlines, heroin made fortunes.

The Rizzutos, through their Sicilian network, tapped into Turkish and Afghan heroin lines. Smuggled via Eastern Europe, routed through Italy, and packed into shipping containers that passed through Belgian and Croatian ports, the heroin arrived hidden in hollowed-out tiles, statues, even frozen meat. Open it up, and you had pure powder that could bankroll a small country.

Hashish, meanwhile, flowed in from Lebanon's Bekaa Valley. Old Maronite connections dating back to Nicolo Rizzuto's era. It was lighter, cheaper, and wildly profitable. Some of it came by sea. Some through private jets touching down at backwater airports where nobody checked manifests too close.

In the chaos of post-Soviet Eastern Europe, warlords weren't just looking for drugs. They were selling guns. And the Brotherhood was buying. AK-47s. Makarovs. C-4. Even RPGs. Cash or coke, didn't matter. Smugglers in Slovenia, Croatia, and Serbia moved crates of weapons through Hamburg and Rotterdam ports, slipped into Quebec through Vermont backroads or Ontario border posts. Some guns went to clubhouse basements. Some got flipped to street gangs. Some made their way south to cartels. Everybody got a taste.

The Rizzutos had forged deep ties with Colombian cartels. They didn't just buy from Medellín or Cali. They brokered. They provided the North American landing pad. In return, they received bulk rates and exclusive routes nobody else could touch. It wasn't just a crime ring. It was an arms dealer with a delivery system.

Even their movements were industrialized. Private charter planes, filed under tourist packages, loaded with dope or cash. Container reroutes, using port insiders to "lose" and later "find" drug shipments. Encrypted communications, using burners with rotating SIMs. Codes layered in seemingly benign text messages that looked like grocery lists. Nobody knew the whole picture. Couriers carried cash, drivers hauled loads, each piece blind to the bigger play. If Halifax lost a shipment? There were three more headed to Toronto, Montreal, and St. John's, each with different handlers, routes, and fail-safes.

It wasn't just organized crime. It was organized industry. A shadow government with better discipline.

From there, the Angels took over.

They were the muscle on wheels. The distributors. The drivers. The collectors. They moved product across provinces and into the U.S., using clubhouses as warehouses and truckers as couriers. They kept order in the streets, taxed every independent dealer, and crushed any challenger with fire and fists.

Once they locked down the routes, it was over. Trucking lines were theirs. Independents either paid their tax or paid in blood. Western Canada opened up like a gold rush.

Vancouver, Calgary, Winnipeg. Every city became part of the grid. Even the U.S. was being tapped. Winnipeg to Minneapolis, Montreal to Boston. Product flowed south. Cash flowed north.

In Quebec, biker towns like Sherbrooke, Trois-Rivières, and Quebec City turned into fortresses. Clubhouses had steel doors, cameras, and lookouts on rotation. Each chapter was its own kingdom. Autonomous, but loyal. They answered to no one but the leadership in Montreal.

Toronto and the GTA, the Greater Toronto Area, was different. The Rizzuto lieutenants controlled the imports through business fronts and high-end brokers. The Angels ran the street game in partnership with puppet gangs, street-level dealers that were taxed, monitored, and used like subsidiaries.

Out west, the payoff was insane. Calgary and Vancouver were cash machines. Meth labs popped up in the B.C. mountains while coke rolled in by truck from Quebec and Alberta. The Mafia presence was quiet but present, investment firms, condo flips, and money-laundering fronts, but they took their cut.

The Angels built an infrastructure of their own. Biker bars doubling as weigh stations. Tattoo parlors hiding burners and safe codes. Trucking companies turned into rolling vaults. They wore leather, but they thought like Wall Street, only their balance sheets were written in cash, blood, and cocaine.

This wasn't a handshake deal. It was a playbook.

The pipeline ran like clockwork. Montreal to Toronto. Toronto to Winnipeg. Winnipeg to Vancouver. Stops in between handled by trusted operators with coded instructions. Each zone had a cash collection point. Money was washed through real estate, hospitality, car dealerships, and shell companies. Loans were made with 10% weekly *vigorish*, interest a borrower owes on top of the principal. In mob slang, "the vig is running" means the clock's ticking, the interest is climbing, and if you don't pay, somebody's coming to collect, politely at first, and violently if you stall.

Every region had a designated liaison. Revenue splits were structured like profit shares. If the Rizzutos provided the product, they took a 60–70% cut. If the Angels sourced their own *Métamphét,* meth, or weed, splits were even or favored the supplier. Laundering fees, protection payments, and enforcement contracts were factored in.

Nothing was left to chance.

And all of it was laundered so clean it could be used to buy condos in Old Montreal. This wasn't mobsters in fedoras. This was suits and spreadsheets.

You don't pull a billion a year and stuff it in a shoebox.

The Brotherhood learned early that power meant laundering. And laundering meant front companies, offshore accounts, and real business mixed with dirty cash.

The Rizzutos used restaurants, trucking companies, and construction firms, often with government contracts. The Angels used tattoo parlors, gym franchises, custom bike shops, and strip clubs. Together, they laundered money through Panama, with lawyers willing to write "clean" books for dirty businesses.

Cyprus and Switzerland had shell companies that "owned" the businesses on paper. Costa Rica and the Dominican Republic were meeting points and safe zones with lax extradition laws. There were homes in Caracas, bungalows in Cabarete, apartments in Miami Beach, each one stocked with cash, weapons, and burner phones. When the heat rose in Canada, the smart ones disappeared down there.

The Brotherhood's greatest trick was making itself look legitimate. The Rizzutos owned restaurants with five-star reviews and celebrity clients. The Angels opened gyms and tattoo shops, hosted food drives, and sponsored amateur boxing events. Construction firms tied to both groups landed public contracts, cleaned money, and employed hundreds, some unwittingly, some very wittingly. They'd built a dual image. Criminals in the backroom, citizens in the front.

The Angels played the public game better. They threw charity rides. Toy drives. BBQ fundraisers for sick kids. They posed for photos. Smiled with local councilors. Behind the leather? Surveillance countermeasures, dead drops, and safehouses. Behind the smiles? Guns, burner phones, and ledgers, all soaked in cocaine.

This wasn't camouflage. This was strategy.

In Montreal, construction wasn't just a trade. It was a racket. The Rizzuto family understood that whoever controlled the unions controlled billions in public funds. *Fédération des travailleurs et travailleuses du Québec*, the Quebec Federation of Labour, or FTQ, Quebec's most powerful labor federation, was ripe for infiltration. The Rizzutos placed loyalists in key union roles. They manipulated job sites, subcontractors, and project approvals.

You wanted the job done on time? You hired their guys. Simple as that. You didn't? The jobsite turned into a nightmare. Delays, smashed windows, workers walking off the job without a word. Materials went missing. Equipment broke. Permits got buried in red tape. The Rizzutos made union politics look like Wall Street hostile takeovers, only with more cement and fewer lawsuits.

And the Angels? They enforced the deals. Bikers walked onto sites in broad daylight, boots heavy, smiles thin. One look was enough. If it wasn't, tires got slashed. Cement mixers got torched. Or worse, someone's kid got followed home from school.

The Rizzutos never posted campaign signs. They didn't need to. They funded politicians quietly through business donations, "consulting fees," and shell firms that made contributions on their behalf. Municipal elections in Laval and East End Montreal were particularly ripe for influence. City councilors found their campaigns flush with last-minute cash. Zoning changes passed quietly. Restaurant permits, real estate developments, and garbage contracts sailed through.

Officials were wined, dined, and flattered. A free trip to the Dominican here. A golf getaway to Costa Rica there. Or sometimes just a thick envelope passed over pasta and veal at an Italian *trattoria*. No one needed to say the word "bribe" out loud. They didn't need to. Everyone understood.

The girls? Yeah, let's not forget about the girls. They kept the money moving and the bosses smiling.

The Rizzutos were never Montreal's kings of flesh. Pimping and running brothels wasn't their bread and butter. But make no mistake, they still got paid. In their world, nothing moved without tribute. Strip clubs, massage parlors, escort agencies, if it was selling sex in the city, it was kicking up to the Sicilians. Weekly envelopes. Monthly "street tax." You could run your own girls, but you ran them under their umbrella. And if you forgot who owned the rain, they'd remind you quick.

Some mob-linked bars and clubs doubled as discreet meeting points where arrangements were made in the back room, away from prying eyes. In the '90s and early 2000s, a few trusted associates ran escort agencies that doubled as drug pipelines, slipping cocaine or ecstasy into the city's nightlife alongside the girls. The Rizzutos didn't usually get their hands dirty running the day-to-day. Those jobs went to street gangs or independents. But the real money, drugs, gambling, loansharking, remained in-house. And the house always took a cut.

The Hells Angels, especially in Quebec, played the game differently. They didn't just collect protection money. They got in the trenches. Through straw owners, girlfriends, and front men, they quietly ran escort agencies, exotic dance clubs, and massage parlors. Sometimes they didn't bother hiding it. Their control went deeper, darker. There were cases tying them to human trafficking rings, importing women from Eastern Europe or South America to work the Montreal sex circuit. And in true biker style, the rackets overlapped, escorts doubled as drug couriers, moving coke or meth to high-rolling clients behind locked hotel doors. The Angels' model was simple. Sell the fantasy, feed the habit, keep the cash flowing.

Montreal. Winter, Late 90s. Snow fell in slow, lazy spirals, settling on the hoods of parked cars like powdered sugar. Crescent Street was alive, a strip of neon in a city of ice. Every door you passed promised something. A drink, a dance, a night you couldn't tell your wife about. The hum of the nightlife was like a pulse, steady and dangerous.

At the corner, *Club Opale* glowed under a crimson marquee. The kind of place where the doormen looked like ex-linebackers and the women looked like centerfolds. Outside, two bikers in red-and-white cuts smoked cigarettes, watching the sidewalk with predator eyes. Leather creaked as they shifted their weight. Their Harleys sat rumbling in the alley, the sound low and patient like they were waiting for something to hunt.

Inside, the heat hit you like a slap. The music was bass-heavy, vibrating in your ribs. Perfume mixed with cigarette smoke. Girls in sequins and stilettos moved like they were underwater, slow, deliberate, making eye contact that felt like a dare.

Upstairs, in a smoked-glass VIP room, two Rizzuto men sat at a small table. Suits sharp enough to cut you, silk ties knotted perfectly. One of them, Tony La Mano, had the calm stare of a man who had done terrible things slowly. Beside him, Luca *"Il Contabile,"* the accountant, the numbers guy, counted bills in stacks of twenties, flicking them like he was dealing cards. They didn't drink much, just sipped espresso and kept their eyes on the floor.

The bikers ran the door and the muscle, taking turns scanning the crowd from the shadows. One guy was a slab of meat with tattoos creeping up his neck. The other was wiry, his face a map of scars and broken noses. They weren't there to smile. They were there to make sure everyone paid, stayed in line, and left when they were told.

The girls? They knew the drill.

Some were from Montreal, others from Russia, Romania, and Brazil, "imported talent," they called it. They danced, they flirted, they whispered prices in your ear. Upstairs, the private rooms had plush couches, mirrored ceilings, and doors that locked from the inside. Anything you wanted, it was here. Anything you could imagine, someone could arrange.

Every tab was tallied, every private session recorded in Luca's ledger. The house cut went into a duffel bag under the table. The split was clean. Half to the Sicilians, half to *Les Hells*.

When a girl went missing for a week, an Angel made a call. She was found in Toronto, working an indie gig. She came back the next day with fresh bruises and no questions. When a drunk stockbroker refused to pay for an hour upstairs, he was walked into the alley. Ten minutes later, he stumbled back in, eyes wide, wallet open.

It was an ecosystem. Predators and prey, all feeding each other. The city knew *Club Opale* was dirty, but it was untouchable. Politicians got free champagne. Vice cops got blowjobs and envelopes. Everyone else got in line.

At 3 a.m., the lights came up just enough to let you know the party was over. The girls disappeared into the dressing rooms. The bikers collected their coats and guns. The mob guys zipped the duffel bag and left through the side door into the cold. Outside, the Harleys growled to life. A black Lincoln slid up to the curb for Tony and Luca.

By the time the sun rose over Montreal, the street looked clean again. But if you knew where to look, you could still see the footprints in the snow, the ones that led from the front door of *Club Opale* straight to the heart of the city's underworld.

And Law enforcement? Please. They weren't overrun, they were bought, bent, or bypassed, right where it counted. At least one RCMP officer was compromised, feeding information about wiretaps and upcoming raids to both Mob and biker contacts.

By now, no one heard the snap when the first crack formed. Empires rarely collapse with an explosion. They rot slowly, from the inside out, hidden beneath marble, behind forced smiles, under piles of money.

The Rizzuto-Hells Angels alliance looked invincible. The ports were greased. The cops were slow. The money was ocean-deep. But deep down, everyone knew golden ages don't last. Especially when the men at the top start looking over their shoulders.

The very scale that made the Brotherhood powerful also made it vulnerable. You can't move billions across borders without leaving trails. And in the quiet offices of the Royal Canadian Mounted Police, the RCMP, Canada's federal police force, Sûreté du Québec, the SQ, the provincial police force of Quebec, who leads major organized crime probes, and the Drug Enforcement Administration, the DEA, the U.S. federal agency specializing in fighting drug trafficking and narcotics-related organized crime, agents had started connecting the dots.

Wiretaps were buzzing. Sting operations were getting bigger. A few low-level guys flipped, then a few more. Police across North America started to see the same names, same companies, same phone numbers, same ports.

And as law enforcement grew smarter, the Brotherhood grew paranoid.

The alliance was still functional, but trust was thinner than ever. The Hells Angels' western chapters began freelancing with Mexican cartels, cutting side deals that bypassed the Rizzuto supply chain. That wasn't business. That was betrayal. Younger Mafia soldiers, less loyal, more greedy, began pocketing more than their share, playing both sides of the street, or cozying up to rival factions.

Vito, always calm, began moving differently. Fewer sit-downs. More intermediaries. He trusted fewer people, and the inner circle tightened. Boucher, too, was restless. His war-hardened lieutenants didn't like the corporate tone things had taken. They were born in chaos. Now they were managers, paper pushers with body counts.

Some liked it. Others didn't. And in between? The kind of ambition that leads to blood.

In late '99, a biker-run bar in Gatineau got hit by unknown shooters. A club dealer with Rizzuto ties was found dead in Toronto, burned alive. Officially, nothing was declared. Unofficially? Tension had a body count again.

Sit-downs grew heated. Intermediaries grew nervous. Even Raynald Desjardins, once a loyal translator between worlds, began plotting his own future. Some meetings were now arranged last minute. Locations changed. Paranoia replaced protocol.

A storm was coming, and everyone smelled rain.

Meanwhile, police surveillance reached a new level. Wiretaps on phones thought to be safe. Bugs planted in social clubs and strip club basements. Informants turned not out of fear, but envy, watching fortunes made while they lived paycheck to paycheck in crime's lowest caste.

Operation Springtime, in its infancy, was beginning to take shape. Prosecutors weren't just going after dealers. They were building RICO-style cases, stacking conspiracy charges like poker chips.

And in those silent courtrooms, the first dominoes trembled.

The success had become a liability. Too much cash drew greedy eyes. Too much territory created jealous rivals. Too many partnerships frayed at the seams. It wasn't a collapse. Not yet. But it was an ending. The golden years were over. And soon, so were the men who built them.

Vito still sipped his espresso in Old Montreal, smooth and unreadable. Mom still strutted outside biker bars, bulletproof beneath his leathers. Deals were still made. Trucks still rolled. Nightclubs still opened. On the surface, the empire was untouched.

But beneath it?

Rot. The kind that doesn't heal.

# Chapter 6

# Blood in the Shadows

The first real fracture didn't come with bullets. It came with whispers. By 2000, money was flowing like liquor at a wake. But as the profits soared, so did the egos and so did the paranoia. Every crate that landed at the Port of Montreal, every brick of cocaine pushed in Toronto or Trois-Rivières, meant hundreds of thousands in street value. And that kind of money demanded one thing. Absolute loyalty.

But in the criminal world, loyalty is like smoke. Everyone claims to breathe it, but it's impossible to hold. The Rizzuto Family had long ruled through diplomacy. Vito was a master of the long game. He solved beefs with strategy, with favors, with leverage. But to Boucher, favors were weaknesses. He believed in tribute. You gave or you got hurt.

That difference showed in how they handled problems. Take the nightclub scene in downtown Montreal. Both the bikers and the Mafia had fingers in the pie. Security. Drug sales. Prostitution. Protection rackets. But when a turf war started between two crews, one connected to the Angels, the other to an independent Mafia crew, Vito sent in mediators. He wanted balance. Boucher? He sent in baseball bats and hammers.

Montreal. Friday night. *Club Soda*. The music was loud, the crowd was packed shoulder to shoulder, and the line outside curled down the block. *Club Soda* wasn't just a place to catch a show. It was a checkpoint. And the two doormen weren't just checking IDs, they were gatekeepers for the Rizzuto crew, low-level associates with more muscle than manners.

On the list? You walked in. Not? You'd better have a damn good reason to be standing there.

That night, the Harleys rolled up slow. Chrome gleamed under the streetlights. A half-dozen bikers climbed off, all leather and patches, the red-and-white Death Head catching the glow like a warning flare. They didn't wait in line. They didn't smile. They walked straight to the door.

The first doorman stepped forward, one of Vito's guys, built like a fridge and just as cold. "Private event," he said. The lead biker didn't answer. He just grabbed the guy by the collar and slammed him into the wall hard enough to rattle the glass. Another biker swung at the second doorman, a sharp, open-handed slap that cracked across the sidewalk like a gunshot. The crowd froze. No knives. No guns. Just fists and presence.

By the time it was over, both doormen were straightening their shirts and swallowing their pride. The bikers didn't even break stride as they walked inside, claiming the floor like they owned it. They didn't have to say a word. It was already written across both doormen's faces. This city belongs to us now.

By the next morning, the whole neighborhood was buzzing. Word moves fast in Montreal's underworld, and this wasn't just a bar dust-up. This was a public humiliation, in front of witnesses, in a spot everyone knew flew under Rizzuto protection. By noon, the street talk had reached Little Italy, Saint-Léonard, and even the strip clubs on Saint-Laurent. Guys whispered over espresso about how the bikers had walked right into a Rizzuto joint and manhandled their guys like rent-a-cops. No respect. No permission.

Inside the Rizzuto camp, the hit to reputation was worse than the bruises. Those doormen weren't just muscle. They were extensions of the family's reach. You rough them up, you're spitting in the Don's face. The old-school guys said it plain. This was a test. The bikers were seeing how far they could push without catching bullets in return. Vito's old guard would've handled it fast. A drive-by, a body in a ditch, something loud enough to drown out the laughter. But this was the new era, and Leonardo's crew was already playing defense on too many fronts.

For the bikers, it was a calculated move. They didn't need to spill blood to make their point. They wanted everyone, dealers, club owners, bookies, to think twice about where their allegiance lay. If the Rizzutos couldn't protect two guys at their own door, maybe they couldn't protect you either.

Vito didn't retaliate.

The meeting went down in the back room of a *dépanneur*, a small, family-run corner store, in Saint-Léonard, the kind of place where the shelves up front were stacked with potato chips and canned soup, but the real business was done behind a locked steel door. Vito sat at the head of the table, sleeves rolled up, espresso cooling beside him. His guys filled the room, old faces from his father's time, and a few young soldiers hungry to prove themselves. Nobody touched their coffee. The mood was tight, the air thick with cigarette smoke and anger.

"They put hands on our guys," one *capo* snapped, pounding his fist on the table. "In front of civilians. Like we're nothing." They saw the Hells Angels not as allies but as parasites. And every incident made the wound deeper. Another chimed in, "They're testing us. If we let this slide, every bookmaker and dope peddler in the city's gonna start wondering if *Les Hells* are the real power now." Vito leaned back, eyes scanning the table. "So, what are you suggesting?"

The answers came quick, too quick. Slash a few tires? No. Burn down a clubhouse? Maybe. Put one of their prospects in the ground? That got nods, but it also meant escalation, a war they couldn't afford, not with the bikers already pressing into their gambling rackets.

One old-timer lit a cigar and spoke up, his voice steady. "You don't answer an insult with a massacre. You answer it with a paper cut they'll feel every fucking day."

That's how they decided. Not a head-on collision, not yet. Instead, they'd bleed the bikers slowly, hit their street corners, shake down their dealers, tax their shipments. Let them know the Rizzutos were still watching, still willing to hurt them where it counted.

By midnight, crews were already moving. Two Angels-run poker games got knocked over. A stash house in Laval got hit and cleaned out. The Sicilians' little raids didn't go unnoticed. By the second night, word had traveled from corner bars in Saint-Michel to the Hells Angels' clubhouse in Sorel. The message was clear. The Rizzutos had stuck a knife in the side of the red-and-white. It wasn't war, not yet. But it was a promise.

Meanwhile, Mom Boucher was getting hungrier. He'd tasted power. The Angels were no longer content to be middlemen. Boucher wanted full-spectrum dominance clubs, ports, distribution, politics. He had already started leaning on construction unions, long considered a Rizzuto stronghold. His enforcers began showing up at job sites. Subtle, at first. Then not. One foreman, a cousin of a Rizzuto lieutenant, had his car torched after refusing to hire a biker-connected concrete crew. The Mafia made calls. Boucher didn't answer. It wasn't just ambition. It was a slap in the face.

Even inside the Angels, cracks were showing. Old-school members in Ontario and British Columbia were uneasy about how loud things had gotten in Quebec. They saw Boucher as a liability. Too brash. Too visible. But Mom didn't care. He had Quebec locked down. Politicians whispered his name. Cops feared his reach. The media called him "The Godfather in a Harley Jacket." And he liked it that way.

Then came a new threat, one neither the Mafia nor the Angels had counted on.

Street gangs.

In Montreal North and Laval, young Haitian and Arab crews were growing fast. They didn't respect the old codes. They didn't play the long game. They were bold, wired on ambition, and armed to the teeth. Many had spent time in juvenile detention centers that served as unofficial training camps in organized crime.

And worst of all? Some were learning from both the Mafia and the Angels. A new generation of criminals, young, disconnected from tradition, began freelancing. Some had done jobs for biker enforcers. Others had trafficked drugs for Mafia-connected lieutenants. But now they wanted a seat at the table. The established powers saw them as pests. But pests with Glocks and no rules are still dangerous.

One night in '01, a crew of Haitian gangsters hijacked a cocaine shipment meant for the Angels. Three men were found in a burned-out van in Longueuil, shot execution-style. The bikers blamed the Mafia for not "securing their end." The Mafia shrugged. "Not our problem," came the reply through intermediaries. But the message was received. The alliance was cracking, and the street-level chaos was seeping upward.

Inside the Rizzuto Family, tensions mounted. Vito's way, diplomacy, and discretion was being questioned. The younger generation, raised in Canadian suburbia but schooled in Sicilian tradition, wanted a stronger stance. Vito's cousin, Paolo Renda, whispered to close associates that Mom was getting out of hand. Even *consigliere* figures like Joe Di Maulo and Rocco Sollecito were uneasy.

Vito tried to hold the line. He believed the alliance still worked for now. But he was also preparing fallback plans. Alternate routes. Loyalists he could activate in a pinch. Silent partners who could move shipments through Halifax or New Jersey if the port ever went hot. He'd learned from history. Power without backup was just arrogance. Boucher hadn't learned that lesson.

Then, the dominoes begin to fall. They always do. In criminal empires, power rarely dies with a bang. It rots. Slowly, from within. From missed payments. From silent resentment. From men who stop being afraid. That rot began in 2000. And it started with a bullet.

Michel Auger wasn't a gangster. Not even close. He carried a notepad instead of a Glock. But in Montreal's underworld, a pen could cut just as deep.

Auger was a crime reporter for *Le Journal de Montréal*, the kind of journalist who didn't flinch when bikers stared him down. But he wasn't just any reporter. Auger had been a thorn in the side of Quebec's underworld for years. He didn't just write about organized crime. He named names. Hells Angels, Mafia, dirty cops, no one was off limits. He published their secrets. He exposed their hits. And now, it was payback.

It was just past 11 a.m. on a warm September morning in 2000. Michel Auger walked out of the office like he had a hundred times before, clutching a stack of notes and a cigarette he never got to light. Auger stepped into his beige Pontiac Sunfire in the newspaper's parking lot, a half-empty lot ringed with steel fencing and office windows.

Then: crack. Crack. Crack-crack-crack-crack.

Six shots, fired at close range. The first round tore through the driver's side window. Another caught him in the stomach. One shattered his shoulder. Bullets punched into his chest and abdomen, ripping flesh, breaking bone. He collapsed against the wheel, blood soaking his shirt, lungs burning.

But he didn't die. Somehow, the stubborn bastard stayed conscious. He reached for his cellphone with shaking hands, fingers slick with blood. Called 911. Voice steady, like he was filing another story. "I've been shot," he told dispatch. Within minutes, emergency crews were on the scene. Auger was raced to the hospital, still conscious, still coherent. The surgeons did what they could, but three bullets were too deep. They stayed lodged inside him, permanent reminders of the price of truth. He lived. Barely.

Police immediately suspected the Angels. But there were whispers that someone in the Mafia may have given the green light or at least looked the other way. The cops launched an investigation. Ballistics. Witness interviews. Confidential informants. Years passed. The case stayed open, but cold. No suspects were ever charged. No one flipped. No one talked. In Montreal's criminal underworld, silence was sacred.

Auger's pen was deadlier than most guns. When he returned to his beat, he didn't flinch. He kept writing. About gangs. About the Mafia. About the Hells Angels. And every time he hit "publish," the streets held their breath. But on the street, the message had already been sent. No one was untouchable, not even a journalist. Auger had crossed too many lines.

But it backfired.

Public outrage exploded. The SQ launched sweeping investigations. Politicians finally stirred. And suddenly, the criminal underworld felt the lights turning on. The bullets that tore through Michel Auger didn't just rip into a journalist's body. They shattered the illusion that the press was untouchable. In Montreal, where ink had always flowed freely, now it was blood pooling in a newsroom parking lot. And the city took notice.

Within days, the streets outside *Le Journal de Montréal* filled with angry voices, not gangsters, but reporters. Journalists, editors, and media workers staged loud, defiant protests, demanding the federal government finally grow a backbone and pass what they'd been dodging for years. A true anti-gang law. Something with teeth. Something like America's RICO Act, the same law that brought down the New York Five Families. The call for change reached Parliament Hill.

Headlines across the country blasted one message: Organized crime had gone too far.

Behind the scenes, Vito was watching closely. Vito wasn't the kind of man who rattled easily. He was a measured, methodical chess player in a world of brawlers. But this was different. The shooting of a high-profile journalist had backfired. Instead of sending fear into the press, it had woken up the government. The cries for a Canadian version of RICO were growing louder, and that terrified Vito more than any rival crew. He knew what RICO had done in the States. He'd watched entire mafia hierarchies crumble, their soldiers flipped, their bosses caged. One good wiretap, one strong testimony, and a whole criminal empire could go up in smoke. Vito couldn't afford that. So, he did what few expected. He ordered the bloodshed to stop.

Behind closed doors, the Mafia flexed its influence not with bullets, but with leverage. Vito reached out to Mom, the man orchestrating a brutal, years-long war with the Rock Machine that had turned Quebec's streets into killing fields. The message was clear. Cool it. The Auger shooting had stirred the hornet's nest in Ottawa. If the heat came down, the whole operation from the port smuggling routes to the club-level cocaine networks was at risk. Boucher, ever pragmatic when it came to money, listened.

September 27, 2000. Quebec City. Inside a courthouse, the unthinkable happened. Boucher and Frédéric "Fred" Faucher, the hardline leader of the Rock Machine, sat down across from each other. Two generals, soaked in blood, with bodies stacked on both sides of the battlefield. The room smelled of sweat, leather, and quiet distrust. It wasn't a peace treaty. It was a business decision. A Mafia-brokered ceasefire, sealed not with a handshake, but with an understanding. There's too much heat and too much money at stake. The Quebec Biker War, which had left over 150 dead and had civilians ducking bullets at daycare drop-offs, was put on ice. For now.

The attempted murder of Michel Auger had nearly killed a journalist. But it also forced the hand of the underworld. And for a moment, the Mafia proved what the public had long feared. They didn't just run drugs or guns. They could influence peace. They could broker war. And they could stop it whenever it suited them. The Rizzutos and the Hells Angels had made billions in the dark. Now the spotlight was burning a hole through their empire.

The police hit back hard. Not with raids but with strategy. They launched a massive covert surveillance project: *Operation Printemps*, Springtime. Wiretaps. Bugs in clubhouses. Informants flipped. Sting operations staged. They went after the bikers first, building a case so wide it threatened to knock out the entire Quebec wing of *Les Hells*. And at the center of it all? Mom Boucher. He was too loud. Too visible. Too addicted to being the face of fear.

In 2002, he was finally brought down. Not for drugs. Not for racketeering. But for something darker, conspiracy to commit murder against prison guards. It was a charge built on betrayal. A former biker had turned informant, and his recordings burned Boucher to the ground.

Enter Dany Kane. Patched up. Wired up. Judas in leather.

He looked like any other biker, leather cut, dead eyes, nicotine-stained fingers gripping the throttle. But Dany Kane wasn't like the others. He wasn't just a soldier in the Rockers, the Hells Angels' bloodthirsty puppet gang in Montreal. He was something else entirely. He was listening. And soon, he would be talking.

Flashback. November '94. Ottawa. The Interpol office gets a call. It's from Kane. Calm, clipped voice. No threats. No bravado. Just a message: "I've got information. And I want to sell it." It was the kind of call that changed the shape of the underworld.

Kane wasn't some nobody trying to shave years off a bid. He was deep inside. Trusted. Dangerous. He knew names, routes, drug weights, shipment schedules. He knew who pulled triggers and who gave the nods. Most importantly, he knew the habits, schedules, and weak spots of the man law enforcement couldn't touch. Mom Boucher. The Nomads' iron-fisted boss. The outlaw king of Quebec. The man who made bullets rain on prison guards and turned downtown Montreal into a warzone. For years, Boucher had been untouchable. Every cop, journalist, and prosecutor in the province wanted his head, but no one could get close. Until Kane.

Now, don't get me wrong, Kane was no angel. Hell no. He had blood on his hands. He'd run guns, moved coke, and helped enforce Boucher's brutal will on the streets. But somewhere between the drug runs and the body drops, he started getting cold feet or maybe just smarter. He saw where things were heading. The war, the heat, the paranoia. Everyone was a target. Even allies. Especially allies. He figured he had two choices. Go down with the ship or jump overboard early and cut a deal.

So, he jumped.

Over the next few years, Dany became one of the most significant police informants in Canadian organized crime history. A ghost in the machine. He fed investigators intelligence so precise it blew holes in the Hells Angels' operations. Clubhouse layouts. Safe house locations. Names of guys who'd never even been suspected before. And most damning of all, he helped build the case that would one day bring down Mom Boucher.

Kane didn't wear a wire because he had to. He wore one because he wanted to. He infiltrated the Angels deeper than any cop ever had, attending meetings, tagging along on hits, talking shop with the highest levels of the organization. All while recording it for the very people hunting them. It was high-risk espionage in the middle of a criminal empire. One slip, one bad read, and he'd be stripped, stomped, and buried in a ditch.

But he kept playing both sides. A ghost to the cops. A brother to the Angels. And eventually, the Judas goat leading Boucher to slaughter. When the dust settled and indictments started falling like dominoes, the name Dany Kane became both legend and warning. To the police, he was a hero. To the Angels, he was a traitor. To history, he was the man who walked into hell, wire under his vest, and walked out holding the keys to the kingdom's collapse.

So, who was this rat, Dany Kane?

He was the devil in a denim vest, a smiling killer in mirrored shades. To the world, Dany was just another soldier in the Hells Angels' war machine, a patched-up enforcer who earned his bones through blood, coke, and chaos. But behind the mirrored lenses was something more dangerous than a biker with a gun. A man playing both sides of the battlefield.

Born and raised in the hard edges of Quebec, Kane was a product of cold streets, busted homes, and a hunger to belong.

He found that belonging in the outlaw world among the Rockers, the street-level shock troops for the Hells Angels' Nomads chapter. If the Nomads were generals, the Rockers were the stormtroopers snorting coke, swinging bats, and pulling triggers on command.

By the mid-90s, Kane was rising fast. He wasn't just muscle. He was smart, methodical, and deadly calm under pressure. Boucher trusted him. The Nomads used him. When something needed to be bombed, shot, or silenced, Kane made the call or pulled the trigger himself. He handled enforcement like a middle manager of murder, keeping the gears turning during Quebec's Biker War, the blood-soaked turf war that turned Montreal into a battlefield between the Hells Angels and the Rock Machine. But all the while, Dany was lying through his teeth.

Starting in '96, Kane became one of the most valuable assets the Royal Canadian Mounted Police ever turned. His codename was "Dunton." And for over three years, he played the most dangerous game in Canadian criminal history. He lived one life in the gang and another in the shadows, feeding the RCMP secrets that would peel back the leather curtain of Quebec's outlaw empire.

He wore a wire. He carried hidden recorders into biker bars, strategy meetings, and murder plots. He sat in rooms filled with killers, nodded at the right jokes, and smiled as they planned executions while silently recording it all.

And what Kane gave the RCMP was gold. Blueprints of the biker war. Dead drops. Drug runs. Internal beefs. The chain of command led straight to Mom Boucher. He spilled everything. How Boucher ordered hits on prison guards to rattle the justice system. How clubhouse meetings disguised murders as internal "discipline." How the lines between biker, dealer, hitman, and cop-hunter had all but disappeared.

Kane was the wire in the heart of the beast.

He gave investigators names, bodies, hiding spots. He helped police map the internal executions that Boucher approved without blinking, cold-blooded purges of disloyal men, often just rumors away from being names on tombstones. He handed over recordings that confirmed suspicions, revealed alliances, and destroyed the myth of biker unity. These tapes became evidence in one of the most aggressive criminal crackdowns in Canadian history.

But Kane never made it to the witness stand. Before he could testify, before the courtroom lights could hit his face, he was dead.

Dany was living on a ticking clock. But the walls were closing in. And Kane could feel it. In July, he got an invitation to a fellow Rocker's wedding. A social event wrapped in leather, whiskey, and suspicion. The kind of place where loyalty was toasted and betrayal could get you killed before dessert. He had no choice but to show up.

The cops, wanting to protect the illusion, handed Dany $1,000 in cash to bring as a wedding gift. Another brick in the lie he was building. He put on the act, smiled for the crew, shook hands, drank with men who'd put bullets in bodies. Maybe he even danced. But the smile didn't reach his eyes anymore. A few days later, the lies caught up with him.

On a quiet street in suburban Montreal, Kane's body was found in the garage of his home. Car running. Doors closed. His corpse slumped like a man who'd run out of roads.

The suicide note was strange, raw, philosophical, fractured.

*"Who am I?*
*Am I a biker?*
*Am I a policeman?*
*Am I good or evil?*
*Am I heterosexual or gay?*
*Am I loved or feared?*
*Am I exploited or the exploiter?"*

It wasn't just a goodbye. It was a scream from inside a man who had lived too many lives for too long. He struggled with personal identity. During imprisonment, Kane realized he was bisexual, a fact he kept hidden. He'd worn too many masks. Killer, informant, friend, traitor. And now, the identities were bleeding together. The line between who he was and who he pretended to be had vanished.

Was it suicide? Or a hit dressed as one? The file stayed open, and the whispers never shut up.

Some say Kane took his own life because the pressure cracked him. He knew the day was coming when he'd be forced to testify, look Mom in the eye across a courtroom, and betray a brotherhood that didn't forgive. Others believe he feared *Les Hells* already knew. That the leather-clad wolves were circling, and death on his terms was better than what they'd deliver. Benoît Bouchard, a key investigator, later said it plainly. "Kane knew his time was almost up. He knew he'd have to testify, and that would expose him as the informant. There was no safe way out."

Dead men tell no tales.

But Kane's wiretaps did. He never made it to the witness stand, but his ghost walked into every trial that followed. The recordings he left behind helped dismantle the Angels' inner circle and put Boucher in a cell for life. He couldn't save himself, but he helped bring down the monster he once served.

In the end, Dany Kane died the same way he lived, alone in the middle of two worlds, neither of which he truly belonged to. The Judas patch burned into his back. The badge buried in his chest. And the truth, still echoing through a garage in Montreal.

Mom never pulled the trigger. He didn't need to. That wasn't his job anymore.

By the mid-90s, Boucher was no longer just a biker. He was a shadow general in Quebec's bloodiest underworld war. He wore his cuts like a crown. He issued orders, not warnings. And when prison guards started dropping dead in '97, Boucher made sure no bullet could be traced back to his hands. But Dany Kane changed that.

Working from inside the belly of the beast, Kane collected the kind of evidence no wiretap alone could offer intent. He exposed how Boucher had turned justice into a target. The murder of Diane Lavigne, gunned down in her car after a shift. The execution of Pierre Rondeau, ambushed while driving a prison transport van. These weren't random hits. They were messages, bullets mailed straight to the heart of Quebec's justice system.

Kane proved that Boucher wasn't just tolerating these murders, he was orchestrating them through layers of loyal killers, including prospects like Stéphane "Godasse" Gagné and Paul "Fon Fon" Fontaine. Kane knew the players, the phone calls, the meeting spots. He gave the RCMP the roadmap. He wasn't just an informant. He was the connective tissue between planning and bloodshed. He drew the line from the trigger man to the throne.

But that wasn't all. Kane's information laid the groundwork for authorities to flip another heavy hitter, Serge Quesnel, a career criminal who knew where the bodies were buried and wasn't afraid to talk. Unlike Kane, Quesnel testified in court. Loud. Clear. Detailed. Quesnel told jurors how Boucher ran his organization like a militia. He confirmed what Kane had recorded in whispers. The killings weren't rogue acts. They were top-down orders. With Kane's tapes and Quesnel's words, the prosecution finally built the unbreakable chain.

And in '02, the chain snapped shut. Mom Boucher, the boss who believed he was untouchable, who had once been cheered like a rock star at boxing matches, who thought leather and fear could keep him above the law, was convicted of first-degree murder. Life. No parole. Game over.

Without Dany Kane, Boucher might've stayed a free man, still holding court in biker bars, still playing god over drug routes and hit lists. But Kane's ghost lived in every piece of evidence. In every courtroom whisper. In every verdict. Kane was one of the most effective informants in Canadian criminal history. He didn't fire the gun. But he gave the cops the ammo.

And that was enough to bury the king.

Mom, the shot-caller who once ruled Quebec's underworld with a grin and a growl, ended up in a cage. And not just any cage. After his 2002 conviction, Boucher was sent to Canada's only super-maximum prison, a concrete tomb in Sainte-Anne-des-Plaines, just north of Montreal. Cold steel and thicker silence. That's where they put the monsters they couldn't control. He was locked inside E-Block, alongside a few of his Hells Angels brothers. But even inside, Boucher couldn't hide. The biker war he'd unleashed had made him enemies everywhere, including the Prairies, the three provinces of Alberta, Saskatchewan, and Manitoba. And now those enemies were in the same building.

August 13, 2002. The walls echoed with steel and rage. A member of the Indian Posse, a brutal, street-hardened gang made up of First Nations members, came at Boucher with a homemade shank, lunging for the man who symbolized white supremacy behind bars. Boucher bled but survived.

But the Indian Posse wasn't finished.

Just a few weeks later, in September '02, they tried to fire a homemade bazooka at Boucher's cell. A goddamn rocket. It didn't kill him, but it sure as hell shook the walls. The prison went on lockdown. Word traveled fast. The wolves were circling, and one of them had a rocket launcher.

Why the vendetta? It went deeper than just the biker war. The Hells Angels have a whites-only policy, no exceptions. And that hardline racism made them natural enemies of groups like the Indian Posse. Earlier that summer, in Stony Mountain Penitentiary in Manitoba, a brawl had erupted when a Zig-Zag Crew member, part of the Angels' network, tossed an Indian Posse member down a staircase. Retaliation was swift and bloody. A Zig-Zag member was stabbed.

Now the Posse's founder, Danny Wolfe, wanted to send a message. Taking out Boucher, the most infamous Angel in Canadian history, would be like planting a war flag on a mountaintop.

With Boucher out of the picture, rotting in prison, the alliance tilted. Vito saw opportunity in chaos. He didn't mourn Boucher's fall. He adjusted.

New Angels filled the void, men like Normand "Casper" Robitaille and Walter "Nurget" Stadnick, hard, seasoned, but more rational than Boucher. They didn't want war with the Mafia. They wanted the machine running again. But the machine had changed. Street gangs were muscling in. The police were everywhere. Customs had tightened at the ports. Corruption wasn't as cheap as it used to be.

Vito doubled down on diplomacy. He reached out to Colombian traffickers directly. He tapped Sicilian cousins to move product through Spain and Africa. He diversified into real estate, construction, offshore accounts.

The alliance with the Angels remained. But it was now a quiet one. No more chest-pounding. No more joint nightclub shakedowns. They shared the same oxygen, but not the same ambition.

And still… trouble brewed.

# Part III: Cracks in the Foundation

# Chapter 7

# The Fall of Vito Rizzuto

December 2003. A chill settled over Montreal, sharp as a warning no one wanted to hear. The sky hung gray, the air thin, and outside a stately brick home in Ahuntsic, all hell was about to break wide open. At precisely 7:12 a.m., a convoy of police cruisers and unmarked vehicles rolled up like wolves around a sleeping giant.

Within minutes, the front door burst open and out stepped the Don. Vito Rizzuto. The man who ran Canada's underworld like a boardroom. Silk tie. Calm eyes. Steel spine. Handcuffed like a petty thief. The charge? Murder. But not just any murder, the triple hit that rewrote New York's mob history. It was pitched as a peace summit, one last sit-down to bury the hatchet. But in mob land, a "peace meeting" often meant someone was leaving in a bag. Or three.

That night, under the low-lit ceilings of the 20/20 Nightclub in Bushwick, Brooklyn, three powerful Bonanno *capos*, Alphonse "Sonny Red" Indelicato, Dominick "Big Trin"

Trinchera, and Philip "Phil Lucky" Giaccone, walked into a trap wearing suits and smirks, thinking they were coming to negotiate terms for the future of the family. Instead, they walked into one of the most infamous bloodbaths in modern mafia history.

This was no random beef. It was the climax of a full-blown internal civil war, a power struggle that had been simmering since the days when Bonanno boss Carmine "Lilo" Galante's murder in '79 left a vacuum the size of Brooklyn. On one side were the old-school hardliners like Sonny Red and his crew, looking to push back against the up-and-coming faction led by Joseph Massino and Dominick "Sonny Black" Napolitano. The family was fractured. Lines were drawn. Guns were cleaned.

The three captains were viewed as a serious threat, too powerful, too independent, and too loyal to the wrong side. Word had it they were plotting to wipe out Sonny Black's crew and seize control of the Bonanno family. Massino and Sonny Black knew the only way to survive was to strike first and strike hard.

So, the trap was set.

The *20/20 Club*, owned by Bonanno soldier Bruno Indelicato, Sonny Red's own damn son, was chosen for the hit. The irony dripped like blood down the walls. They told Sonny Red and the others it would be a private sit-down, just a few guys hashing out differences, mob style. Nobody expected fireworks.

But downstairs, in the club's dingy, windowless basement, killers were already waiting. Salvatore Vitale, Louis "Louie HaHa" Attanasio, and Frank "Curly" Lino, among others.

Men with cold eyes and loaded pistols. Men who'd made peace with what needed to be done.

At 7:00 p.m., the captains arrived. One by one, they stepped into the basement, laughing, confident. The mood was calm. Small talk. Handshakes. No one even raised their voice.

Then came the signal.

Before a single word about peace was spoken, gunfire erupted. In the tight, echoing space, the noise was deafening. Muzzle flashes lit the basement like strobe lights in a nightclub. Sonny Red dropped first, riddled with bullets to the head and chest. Big Trin, all 300 pounds of him, tried to charge, but caught a dozen rounds before hitting the floor like a collapsing building. Phil Lucky was the last to go, frozen in place, shot through the heart.

It was over in less than a minute. No survivors. No hesitation. Just silence and blood pooling on concrete. The cleanup was quick. Sonny Red's body was dumped in a vacant lot in Ozone Park a few days later, half-buried and rotting in his suit. Trinchera and Giaccone? They vanished without a goddamn trace. Their remains wouldn't be found for decades, until the feds unearthed them from a mob graveyard in Lindenwood, Queens, in '04, bones and bad memories buried deep under a building lot.

"The Three Capos Hit" wasn't just a purge. It was a seismic shift. A full-on, premeditated coup that allowed Joe Massino to rise as boss of the Bonanno family and Sonny Black to solidify his power at least for a while. It also marked the dark turning point in the Donnie Brasco operation, as FBI undercover agent Joe Pistone, who had infiltrated Sonny Black's crew, was pulled out soon after to avoid becoming a casualty himself.

Because when *capos* get clipped, nobody's safe, even the buried feel it.

For years, the hit was mob lore, a ghost story whispered over espresso. Everyone knew who'd done it. Nobody spoke. Not until Joseph Massino flipped. The Bonanno boss turned rat, and with him came the dominoes. Salvatore Vitale, Dominick Cicale. One by one, they rolled over. And in their stories, Vito's name echoed.

The U.S. issued a formal extradition request in 2004. Canada complied. The press feasted. For the first time in decades, Montreal's kingpin was off the throne. Vito lawyered up. Charter challenges. Delays. Appeals. But the screws kept turning. And in '06, he was flown to Brooklyn in chains.

In May 2007, facing life and a parade of snitches, Vito did what bosses rarely do. He pled guilty. Yeah, guilty. That's what he said. Straight out.

The sentence? 10 years in Florence, Colorado, a fortress for the most dangerous men alive. No visitors. No freedom. No kingdom. The man who built Canada's Mafia like a Fortune 500 company now ate dinner off plastic trays. The fall was absolute. Montreal felt it before anyone said it. The city changed. Deals grew louder. Meetings turned tense. Guns came out more often. Because without Vito, nobody was safe.

Vito wasn't just a boss. He was the balancing act, the diplomat, the threat, the invisible hand. Every gangster from Park Ex to Palermo knew one rule. Don't move without Vito's nod. Now he was locked up in Florence, and that nod was gone. His father, Nicolo, still alive but slipping. His brother-in-law, Paolo Renda, tried to steady the ship. Francesco Arcadi ran street operations. Rocco Sollecito watched the books. But none of them was Vito. Cracks formed fast. Arcadi's style was muscle over brains, threats, not negotiations. That worked on the corners but burned bridges in the boardrooms. The finesse was gone. And others smelled opportunity.

When Vito was extradited to the U.S. for his role in the infamous 1981 "Three Captains" hit in New York, he left behind more than just a power vacuum. He left behind sharks circling a bleeding empire, and some of the deepest betrayals the Montreal Mafia had ever seen.

Among the wolves was Raynald Desjardins, Vito's longtime No. 2, a man once so close he was considered blood. Alongside him. Giuseppe "Smiling Joe" Di Maulo, a calculating *capo* with old-school ties, and Salvatore "Sal the Ironworker" Montagna, a deported Bonanno boss from New York with ambitions to plant his flag in Montreal. Together, they formed a new axis, a shadow rebellion against the Rizzuto dynasty.

It started subtly. Whispers. Sideline deals. Missed calls. Then the bodies started dropping.

August 11, 2005. Johnny Bertolo. A racketeer, union fixer, and longtime ally of Desjardins, Johnny Bertolo was plugged in deep. Construction money. Kickbacks. Muscle. But when he fell out with Vito, maybe over loyalty, maybe over greed, it was the end of the line. As he walked out of a Montreal gym, bullets slammed into him like punctuation marks in a death sentence. Some say his murder was the trigger, the moment Desjardins turned on Rizzuto for good.

August 30, 2006. Domenico Macri. A feared Rizzuto enforcer, Macri was gunned down in his SUV while waiting at a red light in downtown Montreal. Classic drive-by. Clean. Loud. Daylight. The hitters were close, and they weren't hiding.

September 7, 2007. Frank Velenosi. A loyal lieutenant to interim boss Frank Arcadi, Velenosi was found dead, stabbed and stuffed in the trunk of his Volvo. That was old-school code. Betrayal. Trust no one.

January 15, 2008. Constantin "Big Gus" Alevizos. Another Rizzuto enforcer, Big Gus, had been butting heads with allies inside the family. That kind of friction doesn't last long in the underworld. He didn't make it out.

August 11, 2008. Tony Magi. A construction mogul with Rizzuto ties, Magi survived a murder attempt outside his office. It wasn't his time. Not yet. But the streets were talking, and Magi knew. He had a target on his back.

December 4, 2008. Mario "Skinny" Marabella. Killed as gunmen open fire on him as he exits his vehicle and goes to fill up his tank at a suburban Montreal gas station. No warning. Just a death sentence on four wheels.

January 16, 2009. Sam Fasulo. A top henchman under Frank Arcadi, Fasulo had been maneuvering for position. That earned him a bullet. Montreal was now a *bocce* court soaked in blood.

August 21, 2009. Freddy Del Peschio. A Rizzuto confidant didn't see it coming. He got clipped, another loyalist silenced.

March 19, 2010. Ducarme Joseph. A Haitian street boss and founder of the feared 67s Gang, Ducarme had once been useful to the Rizzutos. But alliances are temporary in the drug game. As he stood in his women's clothing boutique, gunmen stormed in. Joseph lived. His bodyguard, Pete Christopoulos, and a store clerk weren't so lucky. Some said Ducarme had flipped sides, was no longer in Vito's good books, and someone tried to clean that up.

As Vito sat behind bars in the U.S., the city he once ruled like a king from the shadows descended into a war of attrition. His own friends turned into enemies. His own family became targets. The betrayal was personal.

This wasn't just a power shift. This was a purge. Street gangs in Montréal-Nord, wild and fearless, began taking turf like scavengers. Even some Angels, long-time allies, began to question the pecking order.

The balance Vito kept? Gone. Just like that.

The bikers didn't move fast, but they watched. Vito had kept the Mafia-Angels alliance airtight. Mutual profits, clear rules, shared enemies. Now, deals soured. Payments stalled. Meetings grew tense. Some biker factions began cozying up to Desjardins, a man they knew, a man who didn't demand the same kind of loyalty the Sicilians did.

Montreal's underworld, once a web, became a free-for-all. When the first bodies dropped, nobody flinched. But the message was clear. The age of bloodless order was over. This was no feud. It was an extermination. Each murder tore down another pillar of the Rizzuto empire.

The throne was empty, and the vultures weren't on the way. They were already circling.

With Vito rotting in a U.S. prison, Montreal's criminal underworld cracked wide open. The once-untouchable Rizzuto empire, built on *omertà*, bloodlines, and a brutal efficiency, was now a splintered kingdom. And from its broken crown, three power centers emerged, each with a different creed, a different playbook, and a hunger for the top.

Francesco "Chit" Arcadi wasn't subtle. He was a blunt object in a suit. Tough, loyal, and bred from the old Sicilian mold. Arcadi had served as Vito's field general, handling street-level disputes, managing crews, and keeping soldiers in line while the real boss moved silently from the shadows. Now, with Vito locked up, Arcadi was trying to steer the ship through bloodied waters.

At his side stood Lorenzo Giordano, a young, fire-tested soldier who carried out orders with zero hesitation. Giordano didn't scheme. He executed.

Together, they rallied what was left of the Sicilian loyalists, men who still believed in the old ways, the old codes. But belief alone wasn't enough anymore. Not in this new war. Not when bullets started solving boardroom disputes. They had muscle. They had soldiers. But their influence was thinning by the day. Loyalty couldn't patch the holes in their sinking ship.

Then there were the quiet ones.

"Smiling Joe" Di Maulo and Raynald Desjardins didn't roar. They whispered. Veterans of the game, they didn't need to flex because they already had the keys to the kingdom's vaults.

Their power wasn't in the streets. It was in the institutions.

They had ports, control over the flow of cocaine coming in from Latin America. They had construction rackets, the golden goose of Montreal's mob economy. They had political ties and Calabrian backing from the 'Ndrangheta. A colder, quieter mafia that preferred patience over bullets.

Desjardins, once Vito's best friend, now moved with the kind of calculated calm that scared people more than violence ever could. He was the guy you thought was on your side until your car exploded or your nephew disappeared.

This faction wanted a quiet transition of power, a peaceful handover, just not back to the Sicilians. They didn't need to be flashy. They just needed the Rizzuto loyalists to keep dying, one by one.

And then came Giuseppe "Ponytail" De Vito. The wildcard.

A snarling, ambitious wildcard. Younger than the rest, more reckless, more hungry. He didn't answer to anyone, didn't care for traditions, didn't kneel to old dons or dusty codes. De Vito wasn't born into the Mafia aristocracy. He clawed his way up with a crew of loyal madmen, streetwise killers who respected only two things. Power and cash. His operations were crude but profitable. He controlled his own network. Coke, extortion, dirty money, and he moved fast, dirty, and loud.

Where Arcadi sought order and Desjardins maneuvered in silence, De Vito brought chaos. He was the kind of gangster who'd blow up a man's car just to send a message, and if the target wasn't home, so be it. He didn't give second warnings.

He didn't care about alliances. And he wasn't scared of anyone, not even Vito. Some called him the future. Most called him a liability. But in a crumbling empire where trust was a corpse and ambition was loaded with hollow points, De Vito was exactly what the streets were producing now a new breed of gangster bred in betrayal and raised on blood.

Three camps. Three agendas. A Kingdom in Flames.

Arcadi was trying to hold the kingdom together with his fists. Desjardins and Di Maulo were dismantling it with scalpel precision. And De Vito? He just wanted to watch it all burn as long as he got to sit on the ashes.

The only thing they shared was fear, fear of what would happen when Vito came home. Because when he did, the reckoning wouldn't be quiet. The old lion was caged, and in his absence, the empire he built with precision and fear was bleeding out, slow and messy.

Then came the heat. The cops, the raids, the whole goddamn circus came to town. Curtain down.

# Chapter 8

# Law, Order, and Omertà

For decades, the Rizzuto Family and the Hells Angels operated like gods in Montreal, unseen, untouched, unquestioned. Cops chased them, reporters speculated, but nothing stuck. They were whispers in courtrooms, shadows on security cameras, legends in the street.

But by the early 2000s, Canada's law enforcement had stopped chasing shadows. They learned to hunt.

At the front of the pack was the Royal Canadian Mounted Police, no longer the red-coated ceremonial force of postcards and parades. These were federal crime-hunters armed with wiretaps, surveillance tech, cross-border intel, and time.

The RCMP, in collaboration with the *Sûreté du Québec* and municipal police, assembled a new kind of unit. Integrated crime task forces. These weren't about beat cops chasing drug dealers. These were strategic teams. Analysts, undercover agents, wiretap interpreters, cyber sleuths dedicated to unraveling not crimes, but entire criminal systems. They stopped playing checkers. They started playing chess.

It began with whispers and a hidden microphone in a kitchen. *Operation Colisée,* launched in '02, was the wiretap sting that cracked open the Rizzuto Family like a vault. For four years, investigators listened, watched, recorded. Bugs were planted in pasta shops, funeral homes, and the backrooms of bakeries. Mobsters talked. Loudly. Comfortably. Arrogantly.

More than 1,500 hours of recordings, hundreds of hours of surveillance footage. No codes. No filters. Just men talking business over espresso, how to hide cash, who to kill, how to collect. Some conversations were so casual, so confident, it was like they forgot they were in a war.

They caught Vito's right hand, Francesco Arcadi, mapping out territories. They caught Paolo Renda organizing sit-downs. They caught envelopes stuffed with cash changing hands like poker chips. The mafia had always operated in silence. *Colisée* turned their voices into evidence.

In '06, the operation ended in a full-scale sweep. Over 90 arrests, including Renda, Arcadi, and Lorenzo Giordano. The top layer of Montreal's Cosa Nostra was hauled into court broken not by bullets, but by microphones.

Three years later, they came for the Hells Angels.

April 15, 2009. Quebec's criminal underworld woke up to the sound of battering rams. It was still dark when the first door came crashing in. Quiet suburban streets usually reserved for early risers and dog walkers flashed red and blue. Across five cities, the steel-tipped boot of Canadian law enforcement landed hard.

Not a raid. Not a roundup. A decapitation. They called it Operation SharQc, and it was the most devastating strike against organized crime in Canadian history. The numbers alone were staggering: 1,200 officers, including the *Sûreté du Québec*, RCMP, and local police. 156 arrests. 111 full-patch Hells Angels. An empire built over decades, brought to its knees before breakfast. They hit everything.

The raids unfolded like a military operation, surgical, brutal, fast. They hit clubhouses from Montreal to Sherbrooke. Safehouses in the Eastern Townships. Strip clubs on the outskirts of Trois-Rivières. Suburban homes in Saguenay. Storage lockers full of weapons, cash, and secrets. Doors were kicked in. Grown men dragged out in cuffs, some still in their boxers, some still high, most still convinced the badge didn't mean shit.

They were wrong. And about to find out how wrong.

By 9 a.m., Quebec's five major Hells Angels chapters were gutted. Even their puppet clubs, the street-level foot soldiers like the Evil Ones and Rockers, weren't spared.

What followed wasn't just a press conference. It was a declaration of war. The Crown unveiled a case file that read like the script to a crime saga. 22 murders and murder conspiracies. Drug trafficking. Coke, meth, hash, weed. Money laundering. Weapons trafficking. Gangsterism. These weren't petty dealers. These were generals. The blueprint of the biker enterprise, from drug labs in barns to corrupt truckers at the ports, from gun runs across borders to taxation networks on every street corner, was laid bare.

What made SharQc legendary was how deep it cut. Years of wiretaps, surveillance, rat flips, and undercover work culminated in one synchronized, devastating morning.

At the heart of it all sat the Nomads, the crown jewel of the Hells Angels. These weren't just bikers. They were tacticians, killers, logisticians, and racketeers in leather. Formed in '95 by Mom Boucher, the Nomads operated like a shadow government within the biker world. Their Laval clubhouse was less of a hangout and more of a command center. Inside those walls, wars were declared, alliances bought, and enemies erased. They called the shots. They moved hundreds of keys of blow and crystal. They taxed independent dealers, used strip clubs as recruitment grounds, and used trucking companies as drug corridors. They were feared, respected even by the Mafia. And now, they were finished.

Among those arrested that day:

Normand Robitaille, the cold-eyed killer with a bookkeeper's face.

Sylvain Vachon, street-level commander, known for running operations like a CEO.

Michel "Sky" Langlois, one of the founding members of the Canadian Hells Angels, patched in since the '70s.

Though Mom himself was already behind bars, SharQc was his final undoing. The entire structure he built the club within the club was now exposed and bleeding. The Angels thought they were legends. Invincible. Unreachable. Feared.

They weren't prepared to be walked into court in shackles, heads down, colors stripped, surrounded by cameras. Their leather cuts meant nothing in the face of mountains of evidence. Their silence, once sacred, was broken by turncoats and taped conversations. Some would walk on technicalities, trials delayed, evidence mishandled, but most didn't. Some flipped. Most went down hard. It shattered the mythology.

The idea that the Angels were too big, too bad, too connected to fall.

That died on that April day.

The Nomads, once the most feared and efficient criminal unit in Quebec, were history. Their Laval fortress, once a hive of backroom deals, cocaine negotiations, and blood pacts, was sealed shut. The metal doors locked. The cameras unplugged. The place that once pulsed with power was now a crime scene under floodlights.

Their leadership was shattered.

Dozens of Nomads were behind bars, faces drained, still wearing the arrogance they hadn't yet realized no longer applied. Others were scattered on the run, off the radar, or already buried by betrayals. The intricate chain of command so meticulously built by Boucher collapsed overnight. Orders stopped flowing. Tribute dried up. Fear was no longer a currency. Quebec's criminal ecosystem, once tightly wound around the Angels' grip, descended into chaos.

Suddenly, there were no shot-callers to resolve disputes, no bagmen to collect dues, no killers to enforce codes. Drug runners didn't know who to pay. Independent dealers refused to be taxed. Territories became battlegrounds, not businesses. And every hustler, thug, and trigger-happy wannabe sensed opportunity.

Power was up for grabs, but the vacuum was radioactive. Even within the remaining Hells Angels chapters, confusion ruled. Some lower-tier charters, guys who wore the patch but weren't part of the Nomads' inner circle, tried to fill the void. They moved in fast, trying to reclaim turf, shake down dealers, call in old favors. But they were moving under a microscope, and federal surveillance was everywhere.

Phones were tapped. Bank accounts frozen. Clubhouses bugged.

Others pulled back. They scrubbed their names from burner phones. Dumped motorcycles. Went quiet or went clean, fronting like real estate agents or opening mechanic shops that actually fixed cars. Because now, being a full-patch Angel didn't mean power.

It meant a target on your back.

For a long time, law enforcement believed they could never get someone to talk. The code of *omertà*, the Mafia's sacred vow of silence, was ironclad. The Hells Angels had their own version, sealed in blood and patches. But greed, fear, and 20-year prison sentences are powerful solvents.

By the 2010s, the RCMP had a new weapon. Super-informants. Guys like Francesco Del Balso, a former lieutenant in the Rizzuto crew, flipped when the heat got too real. Others followed. Bagmen, smugglers, bikers, guys who knew every dead drop, every stash house, every funeral parlor where a sit-down happened behind closed doors.

They talked about murder contracts, payroll lists, and who sat where at the Sunday dinners. They talked about who betrayed Vito. Who sanctioned hits. Who cut side deals with street gangs. The stories weren't just gossip. They were maps. They rewrote how law enforcement understood Montreal's criminal hierarchy. And they proved something even more devastating. The brotherhood had already broken itself.

As the RCMP listened in and the courts issued indictments, another force shaped the narrative. The media.

Montrealers watched the war unfold not just through crime scenes but through headlines.

*"The Godfather Falls"*

*"The End of les Hells?"*
*"Murder in Little Italy"*

Newspapers like *La Presse, The Montreal Gazette,* and *Le Journal de Montréal* published photo spreads of dead dons, cuffed bikers, and crime scenes marked with yellow tape. Local TV stations ran specials with courtroom sketches and surveillance clips. CBC's W5 and Fifth Estate turned real blood into noir-style documentaries. It wasn't just news. It was theater. The media painted in broad strokes. And the public bought it.

Vito became Canada's Teflon Don, suave, strategic, Sicilian royalty. He dressed sharp. He negotiated peace. He ran Montreal like a shadow prime minister. When he went to prison in the U.S., people waited for his return like a Messiah. When he came back, the city braced for vengeance and got it.

Mom was cast as the villain, a scarred, hulking brute who killed prison guards and ruled the Hells Angels with an iron fist. Boucher was fear personified. His name cleared rooms.

Together, they became Canada's criminal duality. The brain and the fist, the diplomat and the executioner. TV shows, books, and documentaries didn't just report their stories. They immortalized them. But with fame comes fallout. The media spectacle put pressure on cops to deliver results, and they did. Raids, wiretaps, courtroom dramas. Judges threw the book harder when cameras were rolling. Politicians promised justice from podiums.

The underworld watched it all and got nervous. Every handshake became suspicious. Every phone call felt like a wire. Paranoia became policy. Informants were exposed. Snitches were hunted. Some disappeared. Some went into witness protection. Others ended up in ditches. And for all the mythmaking, the real victims, the ones shot for debts, the waiters caught in crossfire, the families who lived in fear, were often forgotten. The spotlight burned hot. And everything under it eventually melted.

Years after the last big busts, the legends remain. Ask a kid in Saint-Michel or Park Extension who ran Montreal, and they'll still tell you Vito's name like it's sacred. Ask an old-timer in Laval about *Les Hells,* and he'll tell you what they did to guys who crossed them, real stories, maybe. Or ghost stories. The mythos of the Rizzuto Family and the Hells Angels isn't just crime history, it's urban folklore. The last great outlaw tale before everything went digital, decentralized, and disposable. Their names linger not just in court transcripts but in rap lyrics, prison tattoos, and barroom whispers. They built empires out of silence. And in the end, it was their own voices that destroyed them.

Across town, the Rizzutos smelled blood. For years, the Angels had been their enforcers, the muscle behind the money. They'd kept the street crews in line, made sure the coke flowed, enforced respect with fear and firepower. But now, the wall of protection was gone.

And the Rizzuto empire, already showing cracks, was exposed. Their enemies saw it. So did their former allies. Everyone with a grudge or an angle started circling.

The Nomads weren't just arrested. They were erased. And in their place, chaos. What rose from that void wouldn't be a rebirth. It would be a street war.

And the bloodshed was just beginning.

## Chapter 9

## The Shot That Shook the Throne

Upper Lachine Road, Montreal. A Tuesday afternoon. December 28, 2009. The kind of day when no one expects death. Sunlight glared off windshields. Horns blared. Engines idled. A few guys in work boots smoked outside a construction site. A woman pushed a stroller. Life moved like any other weekday in the city's west end.

Snowflakes drifted down like ashes, the city quiet under a gray sky. Outside Consenza Construction, the Rizzuto Family's office, Nick Rizzuto Jr. stepped into the cold. He was young, clean-cut, the heir to an empire, carrying the weight of a last name that once made the streets whisper.

The street doesn't give you hints. He never saw it coming.

A gunman waited by the curb, face hidden, nerves steady. In this life, the first rule is timing. The second is distance. The shooter had both. He raised the pistol and squeezed.

Crack. Crack. Crack.

The bullets tore through him with precision, quick, sharp, surgical. Nick staggered back, blood blooming against the snow, collapsing next to his car, eyes wide in disbelief as the last breath left his lungs. By the time help arrived, the pavement was slick red, the heir to the throne bleeding out on the curb of his own family business.

It wasn't sloppy. It wasn't rushed. It was designed to send a message. The killer didn't wear a mask. Didn't care about cameras. Didn't care about witnesses. Because that was the point. This wasn't just a murder. It was a statement. An execution staged like theater. In public, in daylight, with Montreal's working-class heart as the backdrop.

In Montreal's underworld, killing a boss's son was crossing a line nobody touched. But that was the point, the line didn't exist anymore.

The kid's bloody body in the snow said it all. The Rizzuto name didn't protect you anymore. The empire was crumbling, and the war had just begun.

Nick wasn't just another mobster. He was the crown prince of the Rizzuto dynasty. Vito had groomed him for years. He was supposed to carry the empire into the next generation, young, sharp, connected, and with a last name that had built empires and buried enemies.

But on that curb, surrounded by the chaos of screaming civilians and shattered glass, the illusion of invincibility died with him. That name, Rizzuto, had once been Montreal's most feared brand. It opened doors, closed mouths, and moved millions. Now? It drew crosshairs.

Within hours, the news hit every café, strip club, and prison cell from Little Italy to Laval. The prince is dead. The wolves are coming. To the Rizzuto inner circle, it was a decapitation by proxy, a warning that no bloodline was sacred, no man too protected. It was a shot fired not just at a son, but at the very foundations of Vito's crumbling empire. Nick had been loyal. He'd carried the family name like armor. But that name was now a magnet for bullets. And the streets knew it.

What happened on Upper Lachine wasn't an isolated act. It was a trigger. The opening note in a symphony of vengeance, betrayal, and blood. A mob war was coming. The Rizzuto Family was wounded. Vito was still caged in a maximum-security cell in Colorado, serving time for his role in the infamous murders in New York. Inside that cell, word of his son's murder shattered him. According to sources close to Vito, it was the only time he was seen sobbing behind bars. He had lost his son, his legacy, and with him, the balance of the underworld shifted.

Montreal had just witnessed the fall of a prince. And in the world of organized crime, when the heir dies, the city burns. If the murder of Nick Jr. was the opening shot, what followed wasn't just fallout. It was a full-scale symphony of death. Each move was calculated. Each kill was surgical. And each body that hit the pavement sent a message. The Rizzuto reign was bleeding out one hit at a time.

May 20, 2010. The Disappearance of Paolo Renda. A clear, quiet Thursday in Ahuntsic. Midday sun washed over tidy front lawns, old trees, and cracked sidewalks. The kind of neighborhood where people nodded to each other from their porches and everything felt ordinary, even if, beneath the surface, the streets were stitched with secrets.

Paolo Renda stepped out of his modest brick home in Saint-Léonard like it was any other day. Grey suit, polished shoes, a tie frozen in the seventies. No bodyguards. No bulletproof ride. Just a seventy-year-old man behind the wheel of a silver Acura TL, like he had been a hundred times before. He played a round of golf in the morning, dropped by the family's funeral home, and called his wife to say he'd grab steaks for dinner. Ordinary moves for a man who lived anything but an ordinary life. Only this time, he never came back.

By 4:00 p.m., neighbors found his car idling on the curb a few blocks away. The driver's door slightly ajar. Wallet in the glove box. Phone untouched. The man himself? Gone. No struggle. No signs of violence. No blood. No broken glass. Just a ghost trail. Renda had disappeared clean, quiet, without a trace. To the average eye, it looked like nothing. To those in the life, the eerie, unmistakable scent of a clean grab, a mob pro's vanishing act.

You see, he was driving along Albert-Prévost Avenue, and he pulled over for what looked like a police car flashing its lights. Only it wasn't the cops. It was a setup. Two men with guns dragged him into their vehicle. In broad daylight, just like that, Renda disappeared.

Renda wasn't just a retiree in a nice suit. He was Vito's brother-in-law, his wartime *consigliere*, his numbers man, his voice of reason. For decades, he'd sat one seat over from the throne, playing position while the rest were scratching on the break. He didn't carry a gun. He carried weight.

Renda's disappearance is believed to be part of a vendetta for the murders of brothers Paolo and Francesco Violi of the Cotroni crime family, who were both murdered in the '70s.

The news spread like wildfire. Rizzuto loyalists froze. Eyes darted. Phones rang. The whispers started fast, and the Calabrians were flexing. Desjardins was moving. Maybe even Montagna had a hand. Others said the bikers helped clean up the mess, bury the evidence, and collect the reward.

Renda's disappearance wasn't just a hit. It was a knife to the Rizzuto foundation, a surgical cut meant to destabilize the whole pyramid. You don't take Paolo Renda unless you're trying to kill a kingdom.

And if that was the first domino, the next one fell fast and bloody.

June 29, 2010. The Execution of Agostino Cuntrera. Late afternoon in Saint-Leonard. The kind of day that made people roll their windows down and let the radio ride shotgun. Families were getting groceries. Workers were punching out early. But on the side of a quiet industrial strip, behind the loading docks of his food distribution warehouse, a storm was already waiting.

Agostino "The Bulldog" Cuntrera stepped out into the summer light like he had a thousand times before. Gray suit. No tie. Business casual for a man whose real office had no walls, just networks, debts, and respect. At 66, he was old-school mafia royalty. One of the last. A made man back when that meant something. He had been loyal to Nicolo and Vito for decades, Sicilian to the core, discreet, patient, calculating.

But in the months since Vito was locked up and Renda had vanished without a trace, Cuntrera's name had started to circulate as the acting boss. The guy trying to hold it all together while the sharks circled. Some said he was trying to restore order. Others said he was a marked man.

They were right.

He was stepping out of his black SUV, headed into what should've been a routine business day. A car rolled past the loading bay. It didn't stop. Just slowed, windows cracked. No words exchanged.

Then came the thunder.

Pop.

Pop.

Pop-pop-pop.

Controlled bursts. Professional. No panic in the rhythm.

Cuntrera caught multiple rounds to the head and chest. He dropped hard, blood blooming through the asphalt. His bodyguard, Liborio Sciascia, a man who'd stood beside him for years, didn't even have time to draw. He went down seconds later, riddled with bullets, sprawled next to his boss in the hot summer dust.

No warning. No chaos. Just cold execution. They disappeared, gone before anyone blinked.

Police arrived at a war zone sealed in silence. No witnesses. No one had seen a thing, at least not officially. But word traveled fast. Another Rizzuto loyalist, erased in broad daylight. A man who had helped build the empire now gunned down like a street soldier.

Whoever was orchestrating the Rizzuto Family's collapse wasn't shooting blind. They were slicing through the ranks, one capo at a time. Clean. Precise. Remorseless. And with Cuntrera's blood soaking into the concrete, Montreal's underworld felt the tremor.

That warehouse had once hosted BBQs and backroom deals. Now, it was a killing ground. This wasn't gangland chaos. These were surgical eliminations, a purge. The old guard was being hunted. These hits weren't random. They weren't personal. They were part of a blueprint. A cold, deliberate dismantling of the Rizzuto command chain.

One by one, the names that had propped up the empire, Nick Jr., Renda, and Cuntrera, were erased like chalk from a board. The killers weren't spraying bullets in nightclubs. They were hitting in broad daylight, calm neighborhoods, familiar places. They knew the routines. They understood the mindset.

In the aftermath, paranoia spread like wildfire. Old alliances splintered. Safehouses were abandoned. Guys stopped answering their phones. Associates vanished from social clubs and restaurants. Nobody knew where the next bullet was coming from or who was pulling the trigger. The streets went quiet, but not peaceful. It was the quiet of shifting loyalties, of men watching their backs and plotting their exits.

Because if Renda could vanish…

If Cuntrera could be lit up like a nobody…

And the boss's son is clipped…

Then the empire Vito had built the kingdom of suits and silence, of blood oaths and gold chains, was coming apart brick by bloody brick.

In the old days, there were rules. Lines you didn't cross. Sons were off-limits. *Consiglieres* were respected. Hits were rare, strategic, and whispered about in code.

Now? Now, corpses were making statements. It wasn't just about money anymore. It was about revenge, resentment, raw power. Montreal's underworld had cracked open, and the poison was spreading fast.

Even Raynald Desjardins, once a trusted Rizzuto ally, now a rogue general, was playing his own game. His ambitions simmered beneath the surface, and when Salvatore Montagna, a deported Bonanno boss trying to plant a flag in Montreal, showed up sniffing for control, Desjardins helped orchestrate his murder too. No one was safe.

Old friendships meant nothing. Blood ties were irrelevant. You were either a piece on the board or you were being swept off it. In the shadows of this chaos, another virus took hold. Fear. Lower-level operatives started flipping. Guys who used to swear oaths in dimly lit basements were suddenly raising their right hands in courtrooms, pointing fingers.

The old rule "*omertà*" had cracked. Whispers of wiretaps and plea deals rippled through the streets. Every guy wearing a wire looked just like the ones who weren't. Every phone call could be your last. Every drink in a bar could be your funeral toast. Some informants disappeared. Others were found tied up in trunks or not found at all. Just missing, swallowed by the system they once served. For the survivors still loyal to the Rizzuto name, the world had flipped upside down.

And for the Hells Angels?

It was just the beginning of something bigger. While the Rizzutos bled in alleyways and vanished without a trace, the

Angels were watching carefully, patiently, and with purpose. They weren't mourning. They were recalculating.

Vito's empire had been an umbrella. His diplomacy kept the streets from going full wild west. His alliances were forged in trust and terror. With him gone, everyone looked around for the next alpha. The bikers didn't look. They moved.

For years, the Angels had played the role of enforcers and distributors. They were the street generals, the muscle behind the scenes, moving product, collecting debts, flexing when flexing was needed. In the Rizzuto alliance, they knew their place. But with the Sicilian order collapsing, they saw their opening.

By 2010, *Les Hells* in Quebec were evolving. No longer just brawny dudes in leather cutting lines of ice in clubhouses, they were running like a corporation with patches. Chapter presidents became regional directors. Drug operations were mapped like trade routes. Their lawyers were sharp, their accountants sharper.

In places like Laval, the South Shore, and Sherbrooke, the Angels weren't just asserting control. They were replacing what the Mafia used to run. They no longer asked permission. The Port of Montreal, once a Rizzuto kingdom of invisible cranes and bribed customs agents, was increasingly under biker control. They had people on the docks, people in the unions, people on the inside. And they weren't just handling Mafia shipments anymore. Mexican cartels, Colombian outfits, even European suppliers began dealing directly with the Angels. The middleman was gone. The suit-and-tie negotiator was replaced with a guy in a cut who spoke bluntly and paid in cash. Massive hauls of cocaine came in hidden in shipping containers marked as bananas or coffee. Once, the mob helped launder the profits. Now the Angels were doing it themselves through garages, tattoo shops, real estate, and trucking firms.

And they were smart. They still played the outlaw image, riding Harleys, throwing charity BBQs, posing with kids with their brand new bicycles on Christmas. But in the shadows? They were moving weight like warlords. The new Hells Angels weren't alone. They were backed by a growing swarm of "puppet clubs" groups like the Rockers, Red Devils, and Devil's Ghosts, younger, hungrier, and itching for chaos. These guys didn't care about old Mafia etiquette. They weren't raised on *Cosa Nostra* codes. They were born in a world of wireless surveillance, fentanyl, and Instagram flexing.

They started creeping into Mafia turf. They taxed dealers directly. Took over gambling dens. Beat down loan sharks who didn't pay them tribute. They weren't subtle, and they weren't sorry. A bar in Little Italy that refused to buy biker-supplied booze? The owner got jumped in his own kitchen. A strip club with mob protection? Firebombed.

And while the old-school bikers in Laval might've respected the Rizzutos, these new clubs didn't know Vito, didn't care who he was, and sure as hell didn't fear his legend. The alliance that once defined Montreal's underworld had turned into a power tug-of-war. The Angels weren't content being junior partners anymore. The profit split was over. The handshake was broken.

And the Rizzuto loyalists, those still clinging to old titles and dying codes, could feel the shift. The meetings that used to happen in safehouses and backroom *trattorias* were now replaced with missed calls and ghosted sit-downs. The Brotherhood was unraveling, not in a blaze of glory but in quiet, calculated moves. Drug corners flipped. Payoffs rerouted. Loyalty bought and sold. The Hells Angels weren't just outgrowing the Mafia. They were replacing it.

The streets no longer whispered in Sicilian. They screamed in steel and gasoline. Gone were the days of cigar-smoke diplomacy and whispered sit-downs over espresso in Little Italy. Now, respect came at the end of a gun. Allegiance was a moving target. And the city that once bowed to Rizzuto rule had become a roulette wheel of paranoia. With the old Rizzuto guard dead, missing, or hiding, the network, once run like a machine, now moved like a headless beast. Mid-level *capos* scrambled to hold turf. Bookmakers stopped paying tribute. Even street-level dealers started asking, "Who's running the show now?" The answer? No one. Or worse, everyone.

The rules that Vito had enforced for decades, order, silence, discipline, began to crack. Meetings turned hostile. Payoffs got skimmed. Orders were questioned. Allegiances shifted like sand. And in the chaos, the Hells Angels capitalized. They saw the mob slipping. They made their move, slowly at first. Then with teeth.

At first, the fractures were quiet. A mob-linked gambling den in Laval was hit by a group of Rockers. The dealers were told to pay the biker tax or get shut down. A Mafia bagman went missing, his body found weeks later in the Laurentians, hands zip-tied, two bullets to the back of the head. A bar in Saint-Léonard, known to host Rizzuto loyalists, was firebombed after its owner refused to carry biker-supplied booze. These weren't isolated incidents. They were chess moves, strategic jabs testing how far the Angels could go before the Mafia bit back. The Mafia never bit. They couldn't. The fangs were gone.

By 2011, Montreal's criminal underworld was a maze of mistrust. Wiretaps caught mobsters bugging their own goddamn safehouses, suspecting betrayal from within. Even longtime soldiers were subjected to lie detector tests. Some wore hidden wires, either for police or for rivals. No one knew anymore. In one intercepted conversation, a Rizzuto associate told a friend, "If you're not suspicious right now, you're either stupid or fucking dead." No one knew who was talking. No one knew who was next.

Even the Angels, flush with power, weren't immune to the rot. Their puppet clubs, once useful tools for low-level crime, began acting on their own. Some ignored hierarchy. Others openly mocked the Mafia, calling them "dinosaurs," "relics," "suits." The reverence was gone. The alliance was a fossil. A younger Rockers enforcer was heard bragging, "They wore suits and shook hands. We wear cuts and take heads."

Biker lieutenants began expanding rackets without clearance. Clubhouses became hubs for meth labs, human trafficking, and weapons caches. They were no longer playing defense. They were building an empire. An empire with no room for Sicilian honor.

As pressure from law enforcement grew, the code of silence, the old-world *omertà*, collapsed. Men flipped. Not just street dealers, but former loyalists. Made guys. People who'd broken bread with Vito himself. They gave up names. Routes. Safehouses. Port contacts. And with every betrayal, another corpse turned up in a ditch or a parking lot. The underworld was shedding its skin. And all the old tattoos meant nothing now.

It was simple. Get with the new power or get buried.

# Photo Section

Sicilian-Canadian Godfather Nicolo Rizzuto and rival Calabrian-Canadian Boss Vincenzo "Vic the Egg" Cotroni

Surveillance photo of Paolo Violi outside his Reggio Bar, unaware that police had the place "wired" for five years

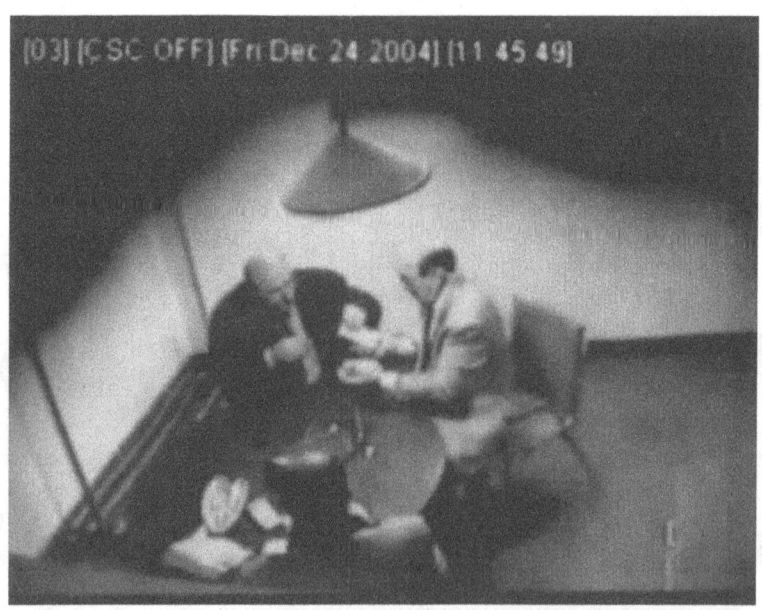

Nicolo Rizzuto, with Rocco Sollecito, caught on tape passing tens of thousands to Nicolo Milioto of Mivela Construction

Vito Rizzuto "Montreal's Teflon Don"

Francesco Arcardi, Pietro "The Lawyer" Triassi, Rocco "Sauce" Sollecito, Nicolo Rizzuto, and Paolo Renda

"Sonny" Barger, taking a break from filming "Hells Angels," on his Harley Shovelhead "Sweet Cocaine" in 1969

Mick Jagger and the Rolling Stones look on as Hells Angels "Security" keep the peace at Altamont Speedway concert

Members of the Popeye Moto Club at their clubhouse before patching over to form the Hells Angels Montreal chapter

Yves "Apache" Trudeau, feared Hells Angels hitman, responsible for at least 43 murders before turning informant

Maurice "Mom" Boucher, the ruthless founder of the Nomads, the Hells Angels' feared Montreal chapter

A bomb exploded Jeep meant for a Rock Machine MC target that killed an 11-year-old boy playing at a nearby school

Walter "Nurget" Stadnick, HA National President in Canada, credited with the club's criminal empire expansion

Mom Boucher, celebrating at a boxing match with Normand "Casper" Robitaille, once a loyal enforcer, later an informant

David "Wolf" Carroll, on the run for over 20 years, with Frank Lenti and Walter "Nurget" Stadnick

"Colors" belonging to Mom Boucher, former President of the Hells Angels' Nomads, expelled from the club in 2014

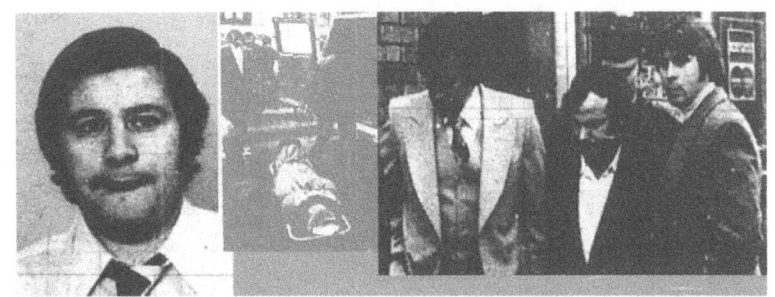
Sebastiano Messina, gunned down exiting a movie theater after Violi linked him to the murder of Pietro Sciara

A month after Vito's return, Giuseppe "Smiling Joe" Di Maulo was executed by a hitman waiting outside his home

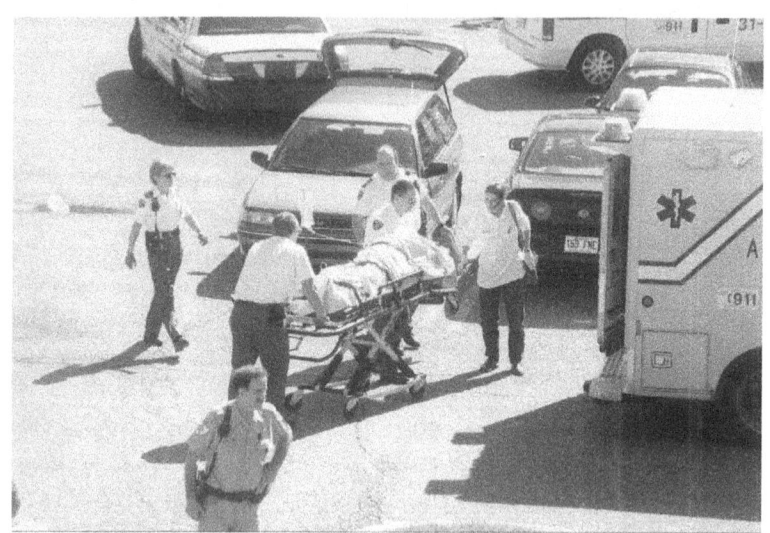

Crime reporter Michel Auger survived a failed 2000 assassination attempt. Six bullets couldn't silence his pen

Frédéric Fauche, National President of the Rock Machine, had brokered the merger with the Bandidos in 2001

Dany Kane (left), the Hells Angels associate who lived as an outlaw by day and a police informant by night

Gambino Captain Gene Gotti and Bonanno Boss turned informant Joe Massino on a walk 'n talk

Surveillance photo in New York City of Gerlando Sciascia, Vito Rizzuto, Giovanni Ligammari, and Joe Massino

"Three Capos Murder"- Phil "Lucky" Giaccone, Alphonse "Sonny Red" Indelicato, and Dominick "Big Trin" Trinchera

The body of "Sonny Red," unearthed in the mob graveyard "The Hole," where Gotti's crew buried him for Massino

Desjardin ally Giuseppe "Ponytail" De Vito, found dead in his prison cell in 2013 from cyanide poisoning

Operation Colisée was a major takedown of the Rizzuto Family, resulting in 90 arrests and over 1,350 charges

Vito Rizzuto's sons, Nick Jr., who was shot and killed in 2009, and his brother, Leonard "The Lawyer" Rizzuto

Agostino Cuntrera, who helped the Rizzuto family gain power, was shot dead outside his food distribution business

Nicolo, here with his wife, Libertina, was accused of hiding $5.2 million deposited in Swiss bank accounts

Nicolo was killed when a sniper's single bullet penetrated the glass of the rear patio doors of his mansion

Nicolo's funeral was held in Montreal's Little Italy on November 15, 2010, and attended by around 800 people

Within a month of Vito's release, the bloodletting began, a dozen men were killed in payback for his family's murders

Francesco "Chit" Del Balso, once a trusted Rizzuto lieutenant, gunned down in 2023 for shifting loyalties

Gregory Wooley was shot dead in front of his fiancée and child, a major violation of the underworld code

Ducarme Joseph, leader of Haitian street gang "the 67s," shot multiple times for his involvement in the murder of Nick Jr

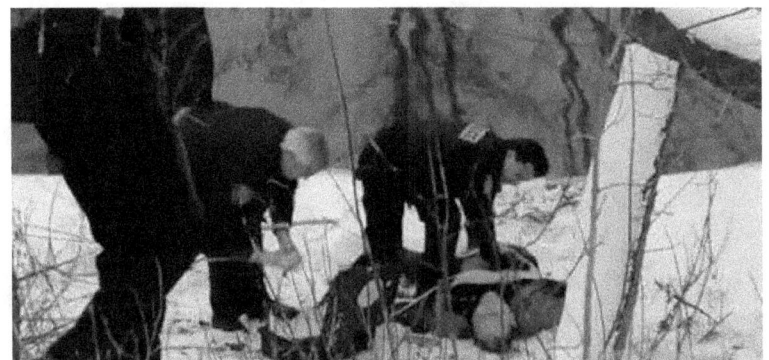

Less than two months after the 2011 failed hit on Raynald Desjardin, "Sal the Ironworker" Montagna was found dead

Mike Di Battista, mob enforcer for Mafia boss Liborio 'Poncho' Cuntrera, is executed in the Dominican Republic

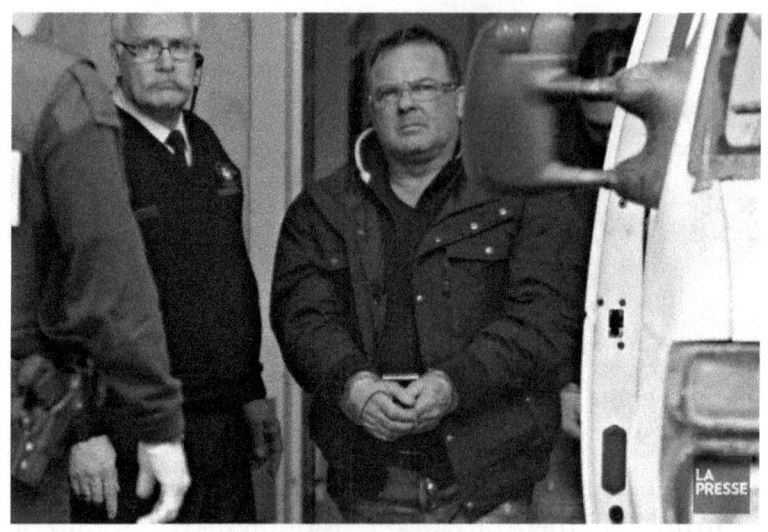

Raynald Desjardins is arrested for his role in the murder of Bonanno Crime Family acting boss Salvatore Montagna

Leonardo Rizzuto, following in the footsteps of his father, Vito, and his grandfather, Nicolo

Martin "Marty the Capo" Robert is one of the most influential Hells Angels in the world

Blood Family Mafia leader David "Pic" Turmel, who carried a $500,000 bounty after Marty Robert put a price on his head

Marty Robert is one of the few Hells Angels who holds the status of "International" member

Vito's son, Leonardo Rizzuto, along with Rocco Sollecito's son, Stefano, believed to be the heads of the Montreal Mafia

Leo's car torn with bullets after the 2023 Laval ambush. Two Porsches with gunmen turned a busy street into a war zone

Pietro "Black Pete" D'Adamo spent months engineering a fragile truce between Leonardo Rizzuto and Marty Robert

# Part IV: Open War

## Chapter 10

## Enter the Street Gangs

The streets of Montreal started whispering a different language, shorter, sharper, and much louder. The old dialects of omertà and patched politics were fading. In their place came a chorus of Glocks and growling engines, a rising pulse that didn't ask for permission and sure as hell didn't bow to tradition.

The Rizzutos and the Angels had ruled the city like feudal lords. Suits in Little Italy, leather and chrome in Laval. They were organized, almost bureaucratic in their criminal code. There were meetings. Votes. Sanctions. Sometimes even apologies.

Then came the street gangs. Young, wild, and ready to take their cut.

They didn't wear suits. They didn't ride Harleys. They wore hoodies and Timberlands, shot rap videos on cell phones, and rolled deep in stolen Honda Civics. Their courtrooms were Instagram stories. Their councils? Park benches and back alleys. Loyalty wasn't etched in bloodlines. It was inked in tattoos and Instagram DMs.

These were the Bo-Gars, the Syndicate, and Master B, names that carried weight in neighborhoods the Mafia never really understood. Montréal-Nord. Saint-Michel. Côte-des-Neiges. Working-class, immigrant-dense, economically forgotten war zones where the government barely showed up, and the cops showed up... late.

But the guns? The drugs? Yeah. They showed up. Early.

These gangs were made in a different fire. Mostly Haitian and Arab kids, second-generation, street-smart, and angry. Their fathers worked in factories or sold cigarettes at metro stations. Their older brothers died young or disappeared into prison blocks. And now, they weren't just surviving, they were hunting. They didn't rise through the ranks. They exploded onto the scene. And the old underworld didn't see it coming.

The Bo-Gars didn't ask for a seat at the table. They flipped the table, took what they wanted, and burned the rest.

At first, the Mafia and the Hells Angels barely blinked. These new punks were useful, ruthless, hungry, and cheap. You could throw them a few bricks of coke, and they'd move it faster than the old distributors. Need someone whacked but didn't want it traced back? Hire a gang kid. No paper trail, no sit-downs, no drama.

For a while, it worked. But parasites grow teeth. The gangs learned fast. If they were doing the dirty work, why take orders? Why split the damn profits? Why kick up to a bunch of aging Italians or fat bikers in clubhouse jackets? Soon, they weren't just working the corners. They were owning them. They weren't collecting for the mob. They were taxing the mob's own dealers. And when the old guard came calling, looking to talk? The response was short. "Fuck talking."

The Bo-Gars started out as a whisper, just neighborhood kids in the late '90s, mostly Haitian teenagers staking out turf in Montreal North, dodging cops, beefing with rivals, slinging small-time dope. They weren't taken seriously at first. No colors, no hierarchy, no reputation, just raw anger and survival instincts.

But by the mid-2000s, that whisper had turned into gunfire. They had evolved into a full-blown urban syndicate. Not a gang. A machine. They were structured, territorial, and fearless. Street crews morphed into command units. Beef became business. And the Bo-Gars started acting like a cartel with the swagger to match. They ran protection rackets on local businesses, charged fees to independent dealers, and had their hands in clubs from Saint-Michel to the East End. Their soldiers wore hoodies instead of cuts. And their code? Answer to nobody. Not the bikers. Not the Mafia. Not even the cops.

Their empire was invisible but everywhere. Teen lookouts posted on half the blocks north of Henri-Bourassa hooded, silent, scanning cars, fingers twitching over burner phones. Every corner had eyes. Every transaction had muscle. And when violence came, it was fast, surgical, and unrepentant. The Bo-Gars didn't care about the old rules. They weren't raised on *omertà*. They didn't toast to the Madonna. They were raised on the street, and they were hungry. For money. For power. For respect.

And the old guard? They were watching the new generation rise and realizing that control was slipping fast.

If the Bo-Gars were fire, the Syndicate was ice.

Born in the shadows of northern Montreal, the Syndicate came up around the same time but took a different path. While the Bo-Gars roared into neighborhoods with flash and fury, the Syndicate moved quietly, calculating, cold. Mostly Arab and North African youth, Moroccan, Algerian, Lebanese, the Syndicate brought a sense of discipline that made them lethal. Where the Bo-Gars were chaotic and explosive, the Syndicate was structured like a paramilitary outfit. Their soldiers wore fitted tracksuits, not baggy jeans. Their leaders drove Audis, not tuner cars. And unlike the bikers or the Mafia, they didn't care about tradition or ritual. They cared about control.

And they got it fast.

They took over entire corners in Parc-Extension, Saint-Léonard, and Côte-des-Neiges. Nightclubs paid tribute. Dealers paid tax. Anyone who stepped out of line disappeared or got lit up in the middle of the street. The Syndicate didn't play games. They used encrypted apps, military-grade weapons, and moved their product guns, coke, meth, even human trafficking like a cartel.

They had roots overseas, too. Money laundering networks ran through Dubai and Morocco. Connections in Europe gave them access to AKs and hash bricks by the crate. The Syndicate wasn't just a street gang. It was a multinational criminal enterprise disguised as one.

And they hated the Bo-Gars.

The beef wasn't just about turf. It was about ideology. The Bo-Gars were loud, unpredictable, and wild. The Syndicate was strategic, surgical, and quietly ruthless. When the war started, it wasn't drive-bys. It was executions. Ambushes outside gyms, cafés, barber shops. A shootout at a Shell gas station became legend.

It went down just after 9 p.m. on a humid summer night, Friday, east end Montreal. A Shell gas station lit up in flickering fluorescence, half a dozen cars idling at the pumps, reggaeton blasting from someone's open window. Then came the first pop. Then another. Then all hell broke loose.

Twenty-seven rounds in under sixty seconds.

Witnesses said it sounded like fireworks until the glass shattered and bodies started hitting the pavement. Shell employees dove behind counters. Customers hit the floor, screaming. One guy tried to crawl under his Civic and got clipped in the leg. Another ran and left his girlfriend frozen by the pump. It wasn't a drive-by. It was a damn execution attempt, two crews trading fire like it was Fallujah, Iraq, during the U.S. invasion.

The streets named it before the papers could. *"The Friday Massacre."*

Security footage caught silhouettes moving like ninjas, hoods up, triggers light. Casings scattered across the lot, mixed in with spilled gas and the blood of a dealer who caught three in the chest. No one ever got charged. No one talked. The word was out by morning. Keep your mouth shut. But for every corner kid or old-school soldier who heard the story, the message was clear. The rules were off. The game had changed. Respect wasn't earned anymore. It was taken at gunpoint, under neon lights, with no warning and no mercy.

By the late 2000s, Montreal's criminal underworld had fractured. The old titans, the Rizzutos, the Hells Angels, were bleeding, locked up, or dead. And in the power vacuum, the Bo-Gars and the Syndicate fought like hyenas over a collapsing empire. Drive-by shootings turned into weekly rituals. Innocents caught in the crossfire. Kids with guns older than they were. The old rules were gone. This was the new Montreal. And the streets didn't care about history, only who held the trigger.

And they didn't knock.

They kicked in the door of a biker-linked bar in Laval like they owned it because that's how they moved now. Fast. Loud. Disrespectful. Five of them in masks. Hoodies up. One with a sawed-off, another with a baseball bat. They didn't come to talk. They came to send a message. The bartender got pistol-whipped. The manager caught a slap so hard he hit the floor. The register was emptied in seconds. And before they left, they tagged the walls in thick black spray paint. Crew symbols. Warnings. War paint.

It was like watching the future spit in the face of the past. These weren't old-school wiseguys or patched-up bikers. These were wolves in sneakers and ski masks, street kids with nothing to lose and no patience for hierarchy. They weren't asking for a seat at the table. They were flipping the goddamn table over.

A week later, another crew rolled up on a mob-connected café in Little Italy. Classic spot. Espresso, checkered table cloths, guys with names like Tony or Sal. Someone inside had told the crew they needed to "show respect" if they wanted to operate in the area.

Their answer came at 3 a.m.

Molotov through the front window. Flames licking the walls. Smoke pouring out into the street like a funeral pyre.

No negotiations. No warnings. Just fire. This new generation didn't flinch at the old codes. *Omertà* meant nothing. Patching in meant less. These weren't soldiers in somebody else's war. They were generals of their own. They didn't want to inherit the throne. They wanted to burn it. The old rulebook? It didn't scare them. They were writing their own. And every tag on a wall, every torch job, every slap across a manager's face was another page in it.

By now, the streets were boiling over. Gunshots echoed through Montréal-Nord like a metronome. Police blotters read like war diaries. Homicides. Drive-bys. Home invasions. Explosions. This wasn't business anymore. It was war. And the old lions were losing ground.

The Mafia had always ruled through presence, the kind of aura that could quiet a room with a name alone. But that power bled out the moment Vito went to prison.

Now their street muscle was being dismantled corner by corner. Mob-connected dealers, guys who used to move weight under the protection of Rizzuto or Arcadi, were getting jacked at gunpoint by kids who weren't even old enough to buy beer. Teenagers with ghost guns and nothing to lose. Hoodies tight. Glock 19s tucked into their waistbands. They didn't ask questions, didn't recognize faces. They just pulled up, put a barrel in your mouth, and took everything. Dope, cash, respect.

These weren't random hits. This was strategic. The shooters didn't care about *omertà*, blood oaths, or the "honor" of the old world. They'd grown up watching their older cousins get buried or locked up for following rules written in another language. They weren't loyal to names. They were loyal to money. And the cuts were better on the streets.

In some cases, it was worse. Sons of old associates, kids raised in mob-linked homes, taught the value of silence and structure were flipping. Selling product for Bo-Gars or Syndicate crews. Why? Because the payouts were fatter. Because you didn't have to kiss rings or sit through a dinner to get made. Because their new bosses were 23, not 63, and they didn't preach tradition, they preached volume.

One former associate's kid was spotted outside a *dép*, kind of like a 7-Eleven or corner *bodega*, slinging coke in his designer parka while his father, a once-feared loan shark, was inside buying lottery tickets and pretending not to see. This wasn't just generational drift. It was a quiet mutiny. The mob had built its empire on fear, on codes, on loyalty passed down like heirlooms. But now? The kids wanted speed. They wanted guns, cash, turf. And they weren't waiting their turn. They were taking it.

One Rizzuto associate, wiretapped by police, summed it up bitterly, "You used to drop a name, and people sat down. Now they look at you like you're speaking Italian."

The bikers weren't faring much better. The Hells Angels had survived the Biker War, but they were getting hit in the pockets now. Street gangs were hijacking meth shipments, undercutting coke prices, and robbing club-run dealers in parking lots.

The Angels retaliated hard. There were beatings, fire bombings, and a few disappearances. But each time, the gangs came back faster, angrier, and better armed. Some bikers tried to cut deals, letting the gangs distribute their product in exchange for a percentage. But loyalty in the streets was fluid. One week's partner was next week's enemy. One disrespect could set off weeks of retaliation. It wasn't just about turf anymore. It was about control. And control was slipping.

For decades, Montreal's underworld had operated on a quiet but absolute set of rules. There were boundaries unspoken, enforced through fear and old-school diplomacy. You didn't touch certain businesses. You didn't kill without clearance. You didn't move product in another man's territory without a conversation first.

Respect? Forget about it. The gangs only cared about cash and corners.

The Syndicate, a fast-rising Haitian crew operating out of Rivière-des-Prairies, began jacking entire shipment lines, including coke coming through port contacts the Rizzutos had cultivated for years. They didn't just undercut prices. They hijacked the supply chains entirely. Dealers who refused to switch over were shot or vanished.

And still, the police couldn't get ahead of it. Why? Because there was no head to cut off. No Don. No table. No fucking rules. Gangs used WhatsApp and Snapchat to coordinate murders. They used PlayStations to communicate, gaming online while plotting hits. They laundered cash through sneaker stores, rap studios, and vape shops. It was organized crime, but not in a way the old players recognized. It was fast, adaptable, and wildly chaotic.

Inside the mob, frustration turned to desperation. Mid-level Rizzuto lieutenants who once walked with quiet confidence were now checking under their cars, wearing bulletproof vests to dinner. The Hells Angels, long used to controlling their puppet clubs with brute force, now found those same puppets turning independent, making their own deals with the gangs, even robbing biker-controlled operations for clout.

The code was collapsing. Younger Angels started calling the Mafia "dinosaurs" behind closed doors. Mobsters started calling the gangs "cockroaches" in wiretapped conversations. But neither insult changed the facts. The dinosaurs were losing the jungle. The cockroaches weren't going anywhere. In less than five years, the power structure that had ruled Montreal for decades was in shambles. The Brotherhood, once a fortress of coordination, discipline, and profit, was now a crumbling tower, surrounded by wildfires they couldn't contain.

Now, fear ruled the streets. Not respect. Not tradition. Just fear. Montreal's criminal underworld, once a chessboard moved by seasoned men in suits and cuts, had become a burning free-for-all. Territory was redrawn daily. Yesterday's enforcer could be today's target. Old alliances meant nothing. Blood meant even less. The city had entered its Wild West phase, and everyone felt it.

Nightclubs paid protection to multiple crews at once, unsure who really ran the block. Drug shipments were taxed three, four times before they hit the street. Gunfire rang out in places once considered neutral. Church lots, school zones, intersections, in broad daylight. It wasn't just criminals dying anymore. Civilians started catching bullets, too. Kids. Grandmothers. Stray rounds didn't care about honor codes.

Cops were overwhelmed. Surveillance units couldn't keep up. The RCMP and SPVM launched joint task forces, but for every gangster arrested, two more took their place. Prosecutors began leaning hard on conspiracy charges and sweeps, hoping to cripple entire networks at once. But most of these gangs were too fluid, too loose. You could dismantle the leadership, and by sunrise, the soldiers had crowned a new boss.

Inside prison, alliances fractured further. Street gangs formed their own power bases behind bars, sometimes controlling more influence than they did outside. Hells Angels kept to their wings. Mob guys kept their heads down. What was once a hierarchy, even in prison, was now a powder keg.

Meanwhile, Vito Rizzuto, locked up in Florence, Colorado, watched the chaos from afar. The empire he built was collapsing. His father, his son, his *consigliere* all gone.

His name still carried weight, but it wasn't the kind of weight that stopped bullets anymore.

# Chapter 11

# Fall of the Giants

The criminal dynasties that had ruled Montreal with iron fists and golden ledgers were unraveling. The city, once a well-oiled machine of mafia discipline and biker brutality, had become unrecognizable even to those who'd built it.

The heat had been rising for years. The city's criminal elite, once united under the iron hand of Vito Rizzuto, was splintering, cracking at the seams like a frozen sidewalk in spring thaw. The old codes were fraying, the alliances dissolving. What began as a whisper in the alleys of Saint-Michel had become an unmistakable roar. The Rizzutos were bleeding.

Montreal wasn't a city. It was a pressure cooker.

The Rizzuto Family, once untouchable, was a corpse with no heartbeat. Slaughtered in a daylight hit. Vanished without a trace.

The hits didn't stop. They never do. Not in this life.

September 29, 2010. Montreal, Quebec. It was just past 3 a.m. when Ennio Bruni stepped out of the *Café Bellarose*, a small bar and social club located in a suburban Laval shopping mall. The neon signs buzzed. The parking lot was full. This was a place people came to drink, eat, flirt. Not die.

Bruni, a mid-level enforcer for what remained of the Rizzuto regime, carried himself like a man who still thought the name meant something. He wasn't flashy, but he had weight on the street he collected, he enforced, and he kept people in line when the bosses were locked up or buried.

But that morning, Bruni didn't see the shooter coming.

Two men in hoodies stepped from a parked SUV. Calm. Focused. Not kids. Not amateurs. Bruni turned, maybe to light a cigarette. That's when the first shot rang out.

Pop. Pop. Pop.

Three slugs to the chest, one to the neck. He collapsed between two parked cars, blood pooling beneath his windbreaker. Panic hit the plaza like a shockwave, customers screaming, people diving for cover, cars peeling out.

The shooters didn't run. They walked.

No one said his name, but everyone knew who it was. Another Rizzuto loyalist down. Another page torn out of the old book. The message was clear. If you still wore the ring, you were a target.

Following the murder, Desiderio "Big Desi" Pompa, Vito's personal bodyguard and chauffeur during his final year on the street, was given the 36-year-old Bruni's gambling and loan-sharking businesses. He was picked up on a bug placed in the *Café Consenza*, the Rizzuto nerve center for decades.

"The .38 is one of the best, you crank it one time, bang, they're dead," he was heard on wire saying in 2008 of his favored choices of weaponry. "The .22 is great, the long one. The .357 short nose, that one's a power. You don't miss, the first shot makes a fucking hole like this, that big."

October 23, 2010. Boucher caught another blade, this time in the prison cafeteria. His attacker was a First Nations inmate who had once tried to join the Hells Angels, only to be rejected for not being white. That rejection festered like an open wound. And when he saw Boucher, the man who embodied the club's racist gatekeeping, he snapped.

Armed with a dining hall knife, the inmate stabbed Boucher repeatedly, yelling about *Les Hells'* whites-only policy as he carved up their ex-prince. Other inmates eventually pulled him off, but not before blood hit the floor.

Inside the penitentiary, Mom wasn't a king anymore. He was a marked man, a trophy target for revenge, for politics, for legacy.

And the hits might not have only come from rivals. Commander Benoît Bouchard, one of the men who hunted Boucher on the outside, dropped a bombshell on the press. "We've heard the Hells Angels leadership in the United States got together and decided to take the fucker out. They say this is the guy who caused all the trouble."

The idea of a U.S. patch pulling Boucher's plug wasn't far-fetched. He'd stirred up too much heat, brought too many headlines. Cops, wiretaps, high-profile hits. He'd turned the brotherhood into a bullseye. And the Hells Angels don't forgive mistakes that cost them business.

November 10, 2010. Montreal. Twilight had just settled over Antoine-Berthelet Avenue, a quiet, affluent street in Montreal's Cartierville borough. But anyone in the know called it something else. Mafia Row. A stretch of manicured mansions, iron gates, and long driveways. Behind those hedges lived the architects of Montreal's underworld: *Capos*, *Consiglieri's*, men who dealt in blood and silence.

Inside one of the stateliest homes on the block, 86-year-old Nicolo Rizzuto stood in the kitchen with a glass of scotch in his hand. He chatted with his wife as she stirred sauce on the stove. It was routine. Comfortable. Safe. He had every reason to feel that way. This was his kingdom.

He was the man who had brought the Sicilian code of *Cosa Nostra* across the Atlantic and embedded it deep into the cold concrete of Montreal. He'd survived the Cotroni wars, outlasted rivals, and passed his legacy to his son, Vito. The name Rizzuto carried weight from Havana to New York to the port of Montreal.

But that evening, something darker stirred just beyond the tree line behind the estate.

A figure crouched in the woods. Dressed in black. Movements slow, disciplined. The kind of pro who knew how to breathe between heartbeats. A sniper. Waiting. Watching. The crosshairs framed Nicolo's silver hair, glinting under the warm kitchen lights.

One breath. One shot.

The window exploded inward. The bullet tore through the glass, through the kitchen air, and through Nicolo's skull. He collapsed before his scotch hit the floor. His wife screamed. His blood painted the cabinets.

And just like that, the patriarch was gone. Executed in his own home, in front of the woman he'd spent a lifetime with. No warning. No guards. No mercy.

There was no getaway car screeching down the street. No spray of bullets or chaos. Just the subtle crunch of boots in fresh snow as the shooter slipped back into the shadows. It was surgical. Cold. Final. And it shattered everything. This wasn't just a murder. This was heresy in the mafia world.

In the old code, you didn't touch the elders. Not at home. Not in front of their wives. Not unless you were trying to burn every rulebook ever written.

But the new wave didn't give a damn about rules.

They weren't toasting saints and kissing rings. They were out for blood, power, and territory. And this hit... this hit was a roar in the silence. Renda's disappearance was the whisper. Cuntrera's killing was the shove. But this, this was the scream that shattered the walls. Nicolo Rizzuto, the Godfather of Montreal, was gone. And every man still loyal to the old regime knew exactly what came next.

No boundaries, no respect, just bodies in the street.

Police, reporters, neighbors, everyone was stunned. Killing a man like Nicolo? In his own home? At that age? It wasn't just bold. It was sacrilegious.

This wasn't about money. This wasn't even about power. This was a torch tossed into the old world, a match to the blueprint that had kept Montreal's underworld in check for decades.

No one was untouchable anymore.

Montreal was catching bodies faster than it could bury them. This wasn't gang warfare. This was an internal reckoning. A mob family tearing itself apart at the seams.

Insiders turning traitor. Outsiders pushing in. Law enforcement knew what they were looking at. A chessboard flipping.

And inside Florence ADMAX, the U.S. federal supermax known as "the Alcatraz of the Rockies," Vito sat in a 7-by-12-foot cell, locked down 23 hours a day. He stared at the ceiling every night, knowing exactly what was happening. Someone was dismantling his legacy, piece by bloody fucking piece.

Vito had once been a king. Now he was just another body in a concrete tomb. The only thing he had left was the past, and in his head. The only thing he could control was his memory. And in that memory, Montreal still belonged to him.

But back home, that memory was being rewritten in blood. The wolves were circling, and they weren't just howling. They were feeding.

If the Rizzuto Family had built the house, the Calabrians wanted the deed. The 'Ndrangheta, rooted in the rugged hills of southern Italy, was patient, methodical, and terrifyingly organized. Where the Sicilians preferred diplomacy, the Calabrians believed in infiltration. They didn't knock on doors. They bought the building.

For years, the Calabrians had been quietly embedding themselves in Montreal's shadows. Not just in the streets but in unions, ports, banks. White-collar crime, drug pipelines, and political lobbying were everywhere, just not loud about it.

And they hated being second-tier.

With Vito behind bars, they saw the opening. The Sicilian regime was leaderless, vulnerable, and fragmented.

Sources pointed to Calabrian-aligned clans like the Di Maulos, the De Vitos, and satellite crews in Ontario. They had waited in silence. Now, they struck with surgical timing.

The plan was simple. Remove the Sicilian leadership, weaken their grip on drug ports and political influence, then slip into the vacuum as "peacekeepers."

But peace was the last thing on anyone's mind.

Raynald Desjardins had sat at Vito's table. He was French-Canadian, not Sicilian, but that never mattered. He was sharp, ruthless, and loyal, or so everyone thought.

But by 2010, Desjardins was done waiting. He wasn't interested in being second-in-command to a man who couldn't protect his own family from a prison cell.

And he wasn't alone.

Desjardins began consolidating power behind the scenes. He kept connections open with Calabrian crews. He whispered in the ears of bikers and brokers. He started reimagining Montreal's criminal architecture with himself near the top.

The hits on Nick Jr., Renda, and Nicolo? Many in law enforcement suspected Desjardins knew more than he ever said. Maybe he didn't order the shots. Maybe he just didn't stop them. In the world of organized crime, that distinction doesn't matter.

Desjardins would later be linked to the 2011 murder of Salvatore Montagna, a Bonanno Family player from New York who tried to insert himself into the Montreal power vacuum. Montagna came with ambition and muscle. He left in a body bag. Desjardins was eventually arrested and sentenced for his role in Montagna's murder. But by then, the damage was done. He had helped tear the Sicilian house down from within.

With the Mob in disarray, the bikers saw opportunity. And the Angels were about to make their move.

The Hells Angels weren't built for subtlety. They didn't care about bloodlines or oaths to Sicily. They cared about cash, control, and chaos.

For years, the Angels had been the Rizzutos' enforcers, dirty work subcontractors with Harley engines and shotguns. But that was changing.

They started leaning harder into narcotics, meth, coke, ecstasy. They made deals with street gangs. They controlled ports, strip clubs, trucking companies. They weren't playing catch-up anymore. They were pushing into territories once off-limits. Loan sharking, gambling, extortion.

Some think the Angels were complicit in the Rizzuto hits. Others say they just watched and waited. Either way, they benefited. The more the Sicilians bled, the more turf the bikers gained.

The old alliance was over. It wasn't declared. It just... died.

The Rizzutos had once ruled Montreal with sophistication and brutality. Now they were outflanked, outgunned, and outnumbered. The wolves had kicked the door in, and they weren't leaving. Everyone in the underworld had a theory. Cops. Reporters. *Consiglieri*. Even doormen at mobbed-up nightclubs.

No one believed the hits were random. No one believed Vito's family was just three more bodies in a city filled with corpses.

These weren't just executions. They were exorcisms.

The question wasn't if there was a conspiracy. It was, which one?

Theory One: The Calabrian Coup

Montreal had always been a Sicilian stronghold, thanks to Nicolo and, later, Vito. But not everyone liked that. Especially not the Calabrians. The 'Ndrangheta had power, real power. Global coke routes. Swiss bank accounts. Influence in Italy's deep state and Canada's boardrooms.

But in Montreal, they played the bride's maid.

For decades, they watched the Rizzutos wine and dine political allies and orchestrate violence with surgical flair. Then Vito went down. And the Calabrians began sharpening their knives.

Theories swirled that they reached out to disaffected Rizzuto men, offering better deals. That they allied with longtime Montreal players like the Di Maulo crew and made promises. "Help us now, and you'll run this city tomorrow."

The hits that followed weren't just about vengeance. They were restructuring. In the corporate world, it's called a hostile takeover. In the Mafia, it's murder.

Theory Two: The Traitors Within

The collapse may not have been engineered by outside forces at all, but by the very men Vito once trusted most. During his reign, Vito ruled like a monarch. He handled disputes quietly, rewarded loyalty, punished betrayal, and kept everyone at the table fed.

But when he went away, the food dried up.

Men like Desjardins, smart, ambitious, power-hungry, weren't content to wait for Vito to return. They saw an opening and made moves.

Others, like Giuseppe De Vito, a Calabrian with ties to both Montreal and Italy, also started shifting allegiances. De Vito would later die in prison, poisoned with cyanide-laced coffee. But while he lived, he was a player in the chaos.

These weren't random betrayals. They were cleansings. Remove Vito's loyalists. Replace them with your own men. Strip the old hierarchy down to the studs and rebuild.

It wasn't a war. It was a silent, strategic *coup d'état*.

Theory Three: The Biker Power Play

The Hells Angels didn't care who wore the crown. They just wanted control of the highways, the ports, the powder. For years, they were comfortable playing the role of muscle, guns-for-hire in leather cuts. But when the Sicilians began falling like dominoes, the Angels started taking more.

Some suggest they supplied intelligence to Vito's enemies. Others believe they backed street gangs in exchange for loyalty and access to new corners. Still others point to the Angels' deep involvement in drug transport, using their network of puppet clubs and international contacts.

Whether they pulled triggers or just benefited from the chaos, one thing's clear. The bikers used the Rizzuto collapse as a ladder. And when the dust settled, they weren't standing in the shadows anymore.

They were on the throne.

Theory Four: Law Enforcement and the Long Game

This one's less romantic but no less dangerous.

What if it wasn't the Calabrians or traitors or bikers? What if it was the cops? After decades of frustration, Canadian and American authorities had learned to fight the mob differently. Not just arrests. Disruption. Wiretaps. Leverage. Informants.

Some in the Rizzuto camp may have flipped quietly, feeding intelligence to rivals or investigators. There's even speculation that some of the hits were preemptive, meant to silence potential rats before they could testify.

The theory goes like this. The police didn't pull the triggers. But they removed the net and watched the sharks eat each other.

Theory Five: All of the Above

The most realistic theory is also the most terrifying. They all did it.

The Calabrians saw an opening. The traitors made their play. The bikers expanded. The cops tightened the screws.

It was a perfect storm. A death spiral. A slow-motion demolition of everything the Rizzuto name once meant. No single killer. No mastermind. Just blood, betrayal, and the weight of too many enemies finally crashing down.

By the end of 2010, Vito's once-tight empire was unraveling in real time. The loyalists were either dead, defecting, or missing. And the sharks were circling. Old alliances with the Hells Angels were weakening. Calabrian clans were rising. Street gangs, once small-time hustlers, were now flush with weapons and ambition. The balance of power was off its axis.

And in the shadows, the man known as "Montreal's Teflon Don" counted the losses from a prison cell, burning with one thought.

Vengeance.

Montreal had seen violence before. But what unfolded in the years following the murders wasn't just another turf war. It was a campaign of calculated destruction. Car bombs. Café fire bombings. Drive-bys in upscale neighborhoods. The city wasn't slipping into chaos. It was diving headfirst.

In previous decades, the violence of the underworld had unwritten rules. You didn't kill in front of families. You didn't shoot near schools. You didn't bomb in the suburbs.

Those rules died with the Rizzuto patriarch.

January 31, 2011. Montreal, Quebec. It was the kind of cold only Montreal understands. A dry, ruthless winter night.

Antonio Di Salvo, a trusted lieutenant of Francesco Arcadi, had just pulled into his driveway in Rivière-des-Prairies. His car's engine was still ticking warm when the first bullet smashed through the driver's side window.

Point-blank. Execution-style.

Di Salvo had spent years in the Rizzuto camp, never front-page news, but a key player in the shadows. He was the kind of guy who got things done. Collections, sit-downs, enforcement. He was Arcadi's problem solver. And that made him dangerous.

Whoever came for him knew his schedule. Knew his routine. Knew he'd be alone, unarmed, tired from a day of moving cash and whispers.

He never made it out of the car.

Neighbors heard the shots, saw the flash of taillights, and called the cops. But it was already too late. By the time first responders arrived, Di Salvo was slumped behind the wheel, soaked in blood and silence. No suspects. No arrests. Just another name added to the growing ledger of Rizzuto-connected corpses.

March 2011. Montreal. It was a quiet cul-de-sac in Laval, the kind of neighborhood where minivans outnumber muscle cars and porch lights flicker after dinner. But just before midnight, peace was shattered.

A luxury SUV sat parked in the driveway of a modest two-story home, sleek, spotless, expensive. Inside the house, lights were off. The street was still. Then came the blast.

Boom.

A fireball erupted like a warzone flashbang. The SUV launched upward, metal shrieking, windows on both sides of the street blown inward. Bedrooms filled with smoke and shards of glass. Toys buried under splintered blinds. Panic in pajamas. Kids screamed. Parents dragged them from their rooms. The entire neighborhood spilled onto their front lawns barefoot, breathless, terrified. The vehicle burned hot and fast, the flames licking toward the sky, a pillar of rage wrapped in orange. Fire crews rolled up too late to save the truck. It didn't matter. It had done its job.

The target survived. A mid-level mob associate with one foot still in the old Rizzuto camp, but rumors had been swirling for months. Whispers said he'd been talking to Calabrians. Meeting with new players. Looking for a lifeboat in a sea of blood. This wasn't a murder attempt. This was a warning shot dressed as arson. And in the Montreal underworld, that's worse than death.

The message was carved in fire and smoke: You can't flip without burning. You can't run without being chased. You don't get to walk away. The cul-de-sac would never be quiet again. And neither would he.

September 16, 2011. Montreal. It was just after noon in Laval, beneath the hum of Highway 25, where the concrete overpass meets the slow-moving current of the Rivière des Prairies. A quiet spot, away from traffic. Private enough for a meeting, public enough to feel safe. Or so they thought.

Raynald Desjardins, now a power player on the outs, sat in the driver's seat of a black Dodge Journey. Beside him, his young enforcer, Jonathan "Jonny the Kid" Mignacca, never far from his side since the war began, tearing the Montreal underworld in two.

They weren't talking business. Not loudly, anyway. Just killing time, watching the shoreline. Then came the thunder.

Crack

Crack.

CRACK.

Out of nowhere, two masked gunmen emerged from the riverbank military-style, fast and fluid. One carried an AK-47, the other a sidearm. No words. No warning. Just pure, surgical violence.

Gunfire tore through the SUV in bursts. Automatic. Relentless. A steel barrage meant not to send a message, but to finish a chapter. Bullets punched through metal and glass, cutting the air like razors. Desjardins caught a few grazing wounds, burns, blood, but nothing fatal.

And then Jonny made his move. Grazed but undeterred, the younger man kicked open the passenger door, Glock already drawn. He fired five rounds in rapid succession, chasing the shooters back to the shoreline. The assailants retreated fast, practiced, coordinated.

And then came the getaway.

With the sound of police sirens still distant, the masked gunmen leapt onto a waiting jet ski, tucked against the riverbank like a getaway car in a heist movie. In seconds, they vanished upriver in a plume of mist and engine smoke, swallowed by the current and the cover of trees.

It was a scene straight out of a mob flick, a waterfront ambush with military firepower, a loyal soldier returning fire, and a James Bond-style escape on water. But this wasn't fiction. This was the real face of Montreal's underworld war.

Desjardins had survived, but only just. And that meant something. Whoever sent the shooters had failed to finish the job, and in a world ruled by reputation, survival was power.

September 2011. Saint-Léonard. Night fell heavy over Café Impériale, a known haunt for old-school wiseguys and under-the-table meetings. The kind of place where the espresso came strong, the wine flowed without a bill, and the walls had ears. It had stood for decades, part café, part clubhouse, part shrine to the fading glories of Montreal's Mafia elite.

Then came the Molotov.

Glass shattered. Fire danced across the linoleum. Bottles of grappa exploded one after another, like a string of grenades. Flames climbed the liquor shelves, kissed the ceiling, and roared through the dining room like a demon unchained. It took forty firefighters to beat the blaze into submission.

No bodies. No blood. This wasn't vandalism. It was a declaration you can't sit in the old booths anymore and pretend the world still fears you.

October 24, 2011. Suburban Montreal. The son of Joe Lopresti, once a key emissary between the Rizzutos and their American cousins, Larry had grown up in the shadow of *La Famiglia*. But he'd drifted, made his own friends, his own enemies. And that night, one of them came calling.

As he leaned on the balcony railing of his home in Montreal's east end, a shooter emerged from the dark and squeezed off a clean burst. Larry dropped before the ember of his cigarette even hit the floor. A life ended on a quiet balcony, no ceremony, no second chances.

Old loyalties meant nothing. Bloodlines? Irrelevant. The streets had turned cold.

November 24, 2011. Charlemagne, Quebec. Salvatore "Sal the Ironworker" Montagna, former acting boss of New York's Bonanno family, deported back to Canada, had thought he could fill the power vacuum. He was wrong.

He tried to seize the Rizzuto empire through alliances and quiet betrayals. But this was Montreal, not the Bronx, and Sal played his hand too fast.

The ambush came like thunder. Gunmen emerged from the trees, cutting off his escape. Montagna ran, sprinting toward the river's edge, feet pounding on frozen leaves, heart racing. But it was no use. He was shot down mid-stride, collapsing into the underbrush, blood soaking into the dirt of a country he barely knew.

December 13, 2011. Back in Montreal. Antonio "Tony Suzuki" Pietrantonio had once stood with the Rizzutos. Now he was labeled a traitor. When the hitmen came, they didn't hesitate. Suzuki took multiple rounds to the body. It should've ended there.

But Tony survived. He stumbled away bleeding, shocked, but breathing. Not everyone got that chance. Whether it was fate, bad aim, or unfinished business, Suzuki lived. But survival didn't mean safety.

Not in this war. These weren't just hits. They were statements. Every explosion. Every Molotov. Every bullet in broad daylight. It was theater with blood for curtains. Burn their cafés. Shoot their sons. Shatter the illusion of control. This was the new Montreal, no *omertà*, no sacred ground, no one off-limits.

If the Rizzutos had built a kingdom on loyalty and silence, their enemies were tearing it down with spectacle and flame. The new killers didn't wait for nightfall. Broad daylight becomes a killing ground.

March 1, 2012. Giuseppe "Joe Closure" Colapelle is silenced. They called him Closure because he had a way of ending things. Disputes, negotiations, threats. But by early 2012, Colapelle was playing both sides, a Rizzuto loyalist-turned-Desjardins insider, feeding intel on Sal Montagna's moves. A double agent in a war with no rules.

They found him dead. A quick and cold hit. No speech. No warning. Just a bullet's final punctuation mark. Closure, indeed.

May 4, 2012. Joe Renda vanishes. No note, no body, no echo. He was a shadow, quiet, careful, connected. Once a loyal Rizzuto earner, Renda had quietly thrown his weight behind Montagna's failed coup. And in this game, betrayal wasn't forgotten. It was filed.

Then, one day, erased. Gone without a trace. Car still in the driveway. Wallet untouched. The street whispered one word. Payback.

June 2012. Notre-Dame-de-Grâce. Midday massacre. A well-known Rizzuto associate stepped out of a gym into a sun-scorched parking lot. It was high noon, families were shopping, kids slurping ice cream.

Then pop-pop-pop-pop-pop.

Five rounds, center mass.

The shooter walked off like it was nothing. No panic. No rush. No mask. Witnesses hit the pavement. A woman screamed. Another dragged her kid behind a car. That wasn't just a murder. It was a message carved in daylight.

July 16, 2012. Walter Gurierrez takes the fall. He laundered money for the Rizzutos, funneled it through fronts, shell corps, and international accounts. A white-collar mechanic in a blue-collar war.

He was walking to his home in the West End when the bullets came, dozens of them. No warning. No chance. He hit the pavement before he even reached the front steps. His crime? Knowing where the bodies were, financially speaking.

August 14, 2012. The Gangs Eat Their Own. First, Chenier Dupuy, boss of the Syndicate, shot dead as he sat in his truck outside a greasy spoon. Windows down. Radio on. Eyes open. Then Lamartine Paul, his second-in-command, executed outside his apartment hours later.

These weren't mob guys in suits. These were street soldiers. Commanders in the street gang army that once served the highest bidder, Rizzutos, bikers, whoever paid best.

Now, they were dropping like dominoes. Some said it was retaliation. Others said it was cleanup. Everyone agreed it was war.

August 2013. Laval. The Tim Hortons Hit. It was just after lunch. A father and his toddler were heading into a Tim Hortons restaurant when the shots rang out. A man tied to biker-led debt collection collapsed just steps from the entrance.

The shooter? Calm. Cold. No mask. The father instinctively shielded his kid's eyes. But the blood, the screams, the chaos, you can't unsee that.

No one wore masks anymore. Not the shooters. Not the gangsters turning on their old crews. Not the businessmen-turned-corpse-cleaners.

In 2012 and into 2013, Montreal's underworld shredded what little honor it had left. The rules of the old guard were buried with them.

Montreal's upper-middle class had grown used to a certain detachment from mob violence. That illusion was shattered. Killings no longer stayed in back alleys or clubhouses. They came to strip malls, gyms, suburban cafés.

The old guard was dead or dying. Nicolo had taken a sniper's bullet through his skull in his own kitchen. Paolo Renda had vanished into the ether, presumed kidnapped and dumped in some unmarked grave. Vito, the last real Don of Montreal, was rotting in an American prison, halfway through his sentence for a decades-old triple homicide in Brooklyn.

The empire they built, with its roots in Sicilian blood and Montreal concrete, was crumbling. And in its ruins, scavengers circled.

There was no single shot that started the war. No formal declaration. But everyone on the street knew the code had changed. Old alliances were just stories. Handshake deals didn't mean shit anymore. This was a new game, and the players weren't wearing silk suits. They were wearing tracksuits, carrying burner phones, and rolling deep with armed crews in stolen SUVs.

From the cafés of Saint-Léonard to the strip clubs of Laval, whispers of betrayal turned into bombings. Shootings weren't statements anymore. They were solutions. Everyone was watching their backs. And in that paranoia, a new breed of gangster emerged.

They didn't call themselves "made men." They didn't kiss rings. These guys were about speed, scale, and cash flow. Crypto, fentanyl, wire transfers, untraceable phones, they weren't playing by the rules. They were rewriting them.

And the old partners, the bikers, the Hells Angels, they weren't having it. They didn't grow up watching their fathers kiss Vito's hand. The new mafia was something else entirely. Born in Canada, raised on Tupac and *Scarface*, they didn't speak Sicilian, and they didn't care about blood oaths. These weren't the sons of the old dons. They were the wolves that survived the purge.

When Vito went down, when the killings started, when the power vacuum cracked open like a chest wound, these guys moved fast. They weren't bound by the old rules because they didn't even know them. And if they did? They didn't care.

They weren't looking for respect. They wanted control.

They formed loose alliances, often more business than blood. Some were connected to the old families' distant cousins, forgotten nephews, overlooked street soldiers, but most had forged their reputations during the chaos. They came up through street-level rackets, drug houses, extortion crews, stolen cars, and built their empires from asphalt, not ancestry.

And they had no problem doing business with anyone who could deliver.

Haitian street gangs, Arab crews from the West Island, Mexican suppliers, and Albanian enforcers, the new mafia didn't discriminate. If the product was good and the profits flowed, it didn't matter who you were or where you came from.

They traded the old-world *omertà* for encrypted messages and burner phones. The sit-downs in *trattorias* were replaced by quick meetings in SUV back seats, warehouse loading docks, and WhatsApp group chats. Their heroes weren't Luciano or Gotti. They were cartel kings like El Chapo or corporate legends like the ones moving fentanyl through China's grey market.

To them, the Hells Angels were part of the problem.

Why split profits with leather-clad dinosaurs still clinging to territory maps drawn in the '90s? Why answer to bikers who demanded tribute but now couldn't protect their own clubhouses from Molotovs? The new mafia saw the Angels the way tech startups see old banks, necessary for now, but not for long.

And when the bikers caught wind of that attitude, the gloves came off.

*Les Hells* had been in this game too long to be ignored. Especially in Quebec, where the Nomads chapter still carried the legacy of blood, fire, and conquest from the Biker War of the '90s. These weren't weekend warriors or tattooed barflies. They were career criminals, soldiers with decades of experience in trafficking, intimidation, and survival. They wore death like a patch on their leather vests.

Guys like Mom Boucher had set the template. Ruthless, disciplined, untouchable. That legacy didn't just disappear when Boucher went down. It lingered in the clubhouses, in the debt books, in the stare of a full-patched Angel posted up at a bar in Trois-Rivières or Drummondville.

The Angels weren't interested in being anyone's subcontractors. That might've flown when Vito ruled the city with charm and fear, but with him gone, the scales tipped. They had their own ports. Their own routes. Their own distribution crews stretching from the Quebec border into Ontario and down into New England. Coke, meth, fentanyl, whatever moved, they moved it.

And they moved a shit load.

But more importantly, they had structure. The Nomads operated like a military unit with regional divisions, coded communication, and layers of plausible deniability. You didn't get to be a patch-holder unless you earned it and survived.

See, when the new mafia started stepping out of line, taxing dealers that the Angels already controlled, muscling into biker bars, refusing to kick up a percentage, it didn't take long for things to get messy.

At first, it was passive aggression. A warning. A stolen shipment here. A missing debt collector there. But when a Hells Angels-owned strip club in Laval caught fire in the middle of the night, things escalated.

Then a low-level mafia associate was found in a ditch outside Saint-Jérôme, two bullets in the chest, one in the face. The bikers had drawn a line. And they were daring the new mafia to cross it. They had built something once.

Back in the days of Vito and Mom, the Rizzutos and the Angels had crafted an uneasy but profitable alliance cemented by mutual enemies, mountains of cash, and a rare kind of respect. They each stayed in their lanes. Bikers ran the street-level heat, the clubs, the enforcement. The Mafia handled logistics, high-end money laundering, international suppliers, and political grease.

It wasn't love. It was business. But now, that business was bleeding.

The handshake agreements made over espresso and rib-eye dinners were ancient history. The men who brokered them were dead, vanished, or locked up. And the new generation, on both sides, wasn't interested in diplomacy. They were interested in dominance.

Every week brought a new incident. A mafia crew jacking a biker stash house. A club enforcer "taxing" a restaurant under a mafia protection racket. One day, a car bomb in Dollard-des-Ormeaux. The next, a daylight shooting outside a convenience store in Saint-Leonard.

Nobody claimed responsibility. Nobody had to. The message was the same every time. Stay in your fucking lane.

The cocaine routes were the biggest battleground. Especially the ones moving from Montreal's port into the West Island, the South Shore, and up the 401 toward Toronto. Whoever controlled those lines didn't just make money. They made power. And neither side was willing to concede even a kilo.

Meanwhile, the victims, dealers, couriers, bar owners were caught in the middle. Everyone had to pay somebody, and if you paid the wrong crew, you might not live to fix the mistake.

Extortion rings crumbled as both sides tried to squeeze the same clients. Bookmakers stopped answering calls. Grow ops burned down. Drug shipments disappeared en route. There was no more honor among thieves, only suspicion, double-dealing, and retribution. The alliance that had once ruled Montreal's underworld like a boardroom was now a battlefield.

And both sides had too much pride and too many guns to walk away.

What made the violence worse was its origin. It wasn't just between rival groups. It was internal. One family faction suspected another of cooperating with police. Longtime allies were now silent at meetings, watching their backs. People vanished mid-conversation, "called to a meeting," and never seen again. The fear was so deep that mobsters began installing armored doors inside their own homes. Guns were kept under kitchen sinks. Old-timers stopped going to social clubs. Wiretaps caught one gangster saying, "I trust my barber more than my *capo*."

Behind bars in Colorado, Vito had time and rage. The deaths of his father, son, and *consigliere* weren't just attacks on his family. They were personal crucifixions. Vito wasn't the kind of boss who forgave betrayal. He was the kind who wrote names down and waited.

Word began to spread. Vito would soon be released.

And the underworld, already soaked in blood, began to brace for what came next.

## Chapter 12

## Vito Returns with Fire in His Eyes

On a gray October morning in 2012, a private plane touched down at Montréal–Trudeau airport. The man who stepped off looked older, leaner. His hair was thinner, his eyes colder. But make no mistake, Vito Rizzuto had come home.

He had spent six years behind bars in a U.S. federal prison for his role in the infamous 1981 triple homicide of Bonanno captains in New York, a mobland purge he had helped orchestrate in his prime. They called it the "Three Capos Hit." It was the stuff of legend. But legends fade. And while Vito was locked up, the empire he built was dismantled piece by bloody piece.

He returned not to a throne, but to a graveyard.

His son had been executed in 2009 outside their family business. His father was shot dead in their kitchen in 2010. His *consigliere* had vanished. Longtime allies had defected or died. And the bikers, once his muscle, were either behind bars or siding with rivals.

What remained was chaos. Street gangs climbing the ladder, drug routes contested by cartels, his own name being dragged through the blood-stained streets of Saint-Léonard. And in true Rizzuto fashion, there were no threats. No press conferences. Just sudden deaths. Bodies in alleyways. Men vanishing without a trace. A quiet war, surgical, symbolic, and strategic.

Vito didn't return to rebuild an empire. He returned with a kill list to burn the traitors out of it.

Between late 2012 and the end of 2013, Montreal's underworld turned into a graveyard of second thoughts. The killings were surgical. Cold. No flash, no chaos. Just bodies laid out like playing cards, each one delivering a message.

The King was back.

First came the cleanup of loose ends. Street-level dealers who'd switched allegiances. Extortionists who'd stopped kicking up. Enforcers who'd once worn the Rizzuto crest like a badge of honor then went freelance when Vito disappeared.

November 17, 2012. Mohamed Awada falls. He was no armchair gangster. Mohamed Awada, a Desjardins associate, had been in the trenches negotiating deals, settling disputes, and taking shots when the bullets flew. But that November night, the crosshairs found him. He was gunned down with precision. One of the few men who knew too much about Desjardins' operations.

December 8, 2012. Emilio Cordeleone gets silenced. Cordeleone was a trusted Rizzuto lieutenant, the kind of guy who didn't say much but moved heavily behind the scenes. He was old-school. Quiet. Reliable. When his body hit the ground that winter day, it wasn't just another mob hit. It was a tear through the foundation.

Rizzuto's circle was shrinking fast.

January 22, 2013. Gaétan Gosselin was gunned down in cold blood. A longtime ally of Desjardins and a respected builder with a portfolio that stretched across Montreal, Gosselin didn't expect to die outside his home. But by 2013, it didn't matter how many deals you made or how clean your hands were if your name was in a crew's phonebook, you were marked. They shot him on the lawn. Left him for the snow to find.

January 31, 2013. Vincenzo Scuderi, another Desjardins man and most trusted lieutenant, was taken out the same way. Execution-style, outside his Montreal home. No one was untouchable, not even on their own doorstep.

May 8, 2013. Juan Fernandez, known on the street as "Joe Bravo," was a heavyweight. A former Rizzuto enforcer turned Ontario crew boss. But his real crime? Trying to stay neutral. He was friends with both Desjardins and Vito. Tried to play diplomat in a war with no peace talks. They found his charred body in a ditch in Sicily, alongside his bodyguard. A burnt offering for his indecision.

July 8, 2013. Giuseppe "Ponytail" De Vito dies behind bars. De Vito was flashy, feared, and powerful, one of the most dangerous Rizzuto rivals still breathing. He ran his crew like a mob CEO from his prison cell. Until one day, he didn't. Poisoned. Arsenic, they said. He died slowly in his cell, clawing at his insides while his enemies toasted.

April 24, 2014. Carmine "The Animal" Verducci gets clipped in Ontario. Verducci was muscle with brains, a rare combo. He ran things out of Toronto, moved weight across borders, and made enemies with the wrong people. One spring evening, outside his Vaughn restaurant, they came for him. Shot down in the street. Not a whisper. Not a word. Just a bloody sidewalk and a lot of closed mouths.

August 1, 2014. Ducarme Joseph's last breath. He was once aligned with the Rizzutos. Then he wasn't. Some even say he played a role in Nick Jr.'s murder. Ducarme ran the streets like a general, ruthless, sharp, connected. But street power doesn't last. They found him dead in the suburbs. No fanfare. Just a bullet and a long memory.

But the real statements came with bigger names.

November 5, 2012. Blainville, Quebec. The leaves had just started to die. The trees were bare, and the wind cut sharply through the north shore suburb of Blainville, quiet, comfortable, upper-middle-class. The kind of place where kids play street hockey and neighbors wave across driveways. But that night, one of Montreal's last old-school mob strategists came face-to-face with the cost of betrayal.

Giuseppe "Smiling Joe" Di Maulo didn't smile much anymore.

He was a relic of the golden era. A Calabrian by blood, but a top *capo* in the Sicilian-dominated Rizzuto family. He was old-school to the bone, conservative, calculating, and quiet. Not the kind of guy who raised his voice, but the kind who made big moves from the shadows. For decades, he stood near the throne. When Vito was king, Di Maulo was one of the trusted few who didn't need to speak loudly to be heard.

But power shifts, and when Vito went down, locked away in a U.S. supermax for a triple murder in New York, it created a vacuum. And Di Maulo stepped toward it.

He aligned with Salvatore "Sal the Ironworker" Montagna, a deported Bonanno boss from New York trying to plant his flag in Montreal. More surprisingly, Di Maulo stood shoulder-to-shoulder with Raynald Desjardins, his own brother-in-law, and Vito's former best friend. Together, they plotted to carve up what was left of the Rizzuto empire. They weren't kids chasing chaos. They were veterans drawing up a hostile takeover.

But Montagna was killed in 2011, after a truce with Desjardins collapsed in a hail of bullets by a riverbank. And Desjardins, once the quiet operator, got sloppy. He ended up in cuffs. Suddenly, the alliance that was supposed to be surgical and smart looked more like a bloody disaster.

That left Smiling Joe standing alone.

Just after dark, Di Maulo pulled into his driveway in Blainville. He lived modestly for a man of his past, no fortress, no guards. Just a man trying to age out of the game. He stepped out of his car, maybe thinking about dinner, maybe thinking about the empire he once touched.

Two shadows stepped out from the dark. No conversation. No warning. Just cold precision.

Crack. Crack. Crack.

Gunshots echoed through the neighborhood. Di Maulo hit the pavement face down, riddled with bullets. His blood pooled across the concrete. A neighbor called it in. Others peeked through blinds, already knowing this wasn't a random act. This was Montreal's underworld cleaning house.

Loyalty doesn't age well.

Di Maulo had played both sides, Rizzuto and then the coup. And now, with Vito back on Canadian soil, the reckoning had begun. The Godfather's return wasn't just symbolic. It was lethal.

Smiling Joe had rolled the dice. He bet against the old lion. And in the end, he died alone on his driveway, surrounded by silence.

July 12, 2013. Woodbridge, Ontario. The night was pure GTA mob royalty. A bachelor party in Woodbridge, just north of Toronto, Bentleys lined the valet, cigars burned in the parking lot, and whispers of business hung in the air between toasts and slow dances.

Salvatore "Young Gun Sam" Calautti was there too, suited up and swaggering. In the Toronto underworld, Calautti was considered next-gen muscle. Fast with his fists, faster with his gun. A street-bred killer with ambitions that stretched from the GTA to Montreal and back again. He didn't just play the game. He tried to rewrite it.

But that night, someone else was holding the pen.

Just past midnight, Calautti and his longtime driver, Jimmy Tusek, stepped out into the parking lot outside a banquet hall. The air was thick with cologne and champagne. The music still thumped behind the glass.

Then came the roar of a vehicle engine. Headlights flared. A black SUV rolled past slow, too slow. A window dropped. And then, chaos. A barrage of bullets shattered the night. Witnesses later said it sounded like a machine gun in a tunnel, over 20 rounds fired in seconds. Calautti was ripped apart where he stood. Tusek didn't have time to react. Glass exploded. Tires screeched. Guests hit the ground in tuxedos and stilettos. The wedding became a war zone.

When the smoke cleared, both men were dead. Executed. No warning. No subtlety. Just blood on asphalt and a hall full of stunned wiseguys who knew exactly what this was.

Payback.

Calautti wasn't just another GTA thug. He was a prime suspect in a string of hits that gutted the Rizzuto Crime Family in the early 2000s. Montreal police believed he had ties to the murders of Nicolo, gunned down by a sniper through his kitchen window, Nick Jr., ambushed in broad daylight outside a Montreal office, and Gaetano "Guy" Panepinto, Vito's Toronto-based *capo*, blown up in a car bomb.

And Calautti didn't exactly deny the whispers. He liked the heat. He dressed like a GQ model, rolled with heavy hitters, and never sat with his back to the door. He once famously said, "If they're gonna get me, I want them to work for it."

They did. And they did it loud.

November 10, 2013. Acapulco, México. The air was thick with salt and smoke. Tourists sipped margaritas and watched the sun bleed into the Pacific. But a thousand miles from Montreal's cold streets, the ghosts of a mafia war were still hunting.

Moreno "The Turkey" Gallo was sitting in an Italian restaurant in Acapulco, white shirt, quiet posture, the kind of man who had learned to keep his back to the wall. He was 68, gray around the temples, but still sharp, still wired to the old codes. He wasn't there for the beach. He was there because Canada had exiled him.

By the early 2000s, Gallo's name started showing up on federal watchlists. The Canadian government accused him of being a major organized crime player and tied him to an unsolved gangland murder. In 2007, his longtime friend and fellow mobster Giuseppe "The Beau" De Vito was arrested. Pressure mounted. Wiretaps buzzed. Gallo became a liability.

In January 2013, after years of bureaucratic tug-of-war, Gallo was officially deported from Canada. Mexico was supposed to be a landing pad. A place to fade. He had family there, some money, and enough street smarts to stay under the radar, or so he thought. And someone had let him believe exile meant safety.

It didn't.

Just past 7:30 p.m., a man walked into the restaurant like he belonged there. No rush. No mask. He moved with the confidence of someone who knew exactly who he was looking for.

He found him.

One shot. Straight to the head. Gallo slumped forward onto the table, blood soaking into the white tablecloth. The shooter slipped out just as quietly. No panic. No screaming. Just clean work and an empty chair.

Gallo wasn't a headline-grabbing mobster. He wasn't a fire starter like Boucher, or a boss like Vito. But he was respected. A Calabrian with old ties, Gallo had once moved in the same circles as the Rizzutos. For years, he operated quietly behind the scenes, mediating disputes, managing business, keeping the peace between powerful factions when bullets weren't doing the talking.

But peace is a currency that dries up fast.

But this wasn't just immigration paperwork catching up to him. This was revenge. Vito Rizzuto was back. And the kill list was getting shorter.

Gallo had been seen by many as sitting on the wrong side of the underworld's great divide. While Vito sat rotting in an American prison, his enemies had tried to carve up the empire. Gallo didn't throw punches, but he didn't stop the fight either. And silence is a form of betrayal.

December 18, 2013. Laval, Quebec. The first body hit the pavement just after dawn.

It was Emmanuel "Dino" Frustaci, street tough, mid-level mover, a guy who played both sides like it was a poker table and he held the cards. But by the end, Dino had no chips left. He was found face-down in the snowy silence of Laval, his jacket soaked through, a halo of red spreading from his chest. Multiple gunshot wounds, tight groupings. Professional. Personal.

He wasn't a boss. He wasn't even top-tier muscle. But Dino had one fatal flaw. He thought he could float between camps in a war where the rules were being rewritten in blood.

Frustaci had danced on the edge of both the Rizzuto loyalists and the Montagna-Desjardins rebellion. He'd run messages, moved product, whispered intel. But in a world that had turned paranoid, volatile, and tribal, where every move was under a microscope, that kind of freelancing was a death wish.

By the time they found his body, it was already clear, Dino had been marked. You were either with the returning King… or you were against him.

December 18, 2013. Suburban Montreal. Later that same day, before the streets could even absorb the weight of Frustaci's murder, the second hammer dropped.

Roger Valiquette, a known associate of "Smiling Joe" Di Maulo and the Gallo camp, was gunned down in broad daylight, no alley, no backdoor setup. This was done loud.

Valiquette was standing outside a nondescript building in a quiet neighborhood when the hit squad rolled up. No words. Just a cold execution, bullets ripping into him before he even had a chance to turn around.

It was surgical. Efficient. And theatrical.

Because Roger wasn't just a soldier. He was a signal. A flag planted firmly on the side of the old-guard traitors, Di Maulo, Gallo, Montagna. The ones who'd made their move while Vito was behind bars in a Colorado supermax. The ones who thought the lion had died in his cage.

The murders of Frustaci and Valiquette weren't random hits. They were part of a purge. Street-level or not, everyone who had whispered in the wrong ears, carried the wrong message, or even sat at the wrong dinner table was now fair game.

In the underworld, there's no statute of limitations on betrayal. And Vito was crossing names off his list. Every killing wasn't just vengeance. It was restoration.

The ports were reclaimed. Cocaine supply chains disrupted and diluted during Vito's absence were rerouted through the old Venezuelan and Dominican channels he once controlled. Customs officials were paid off like in the old days. Trusted middlemen were brought back into the fold.

Construction rackets that had drifted into biker hands were flipped back sometimes through negotiations, often through quiet force. Gambling dens started kicking up again. Loansharking crews resumed collection with renewed precision.

Vito wasn't rebuilding an empire brick by brick. He was blowing the dust off a throne no one had been worthy of sitting in. And if anyone had dreams of resistance, they were reminded of what happened to Sal the Ironworker in Brooklyn. Or Gallo in Acapulco. Or the men found crumpled in parking lots across Laval and Saint-Michel.

This was a resurrection. And the streets fell in line.

By the winter of 2013, the streets of Montreal had gone quiet, but it wasn't peace. It was fear. A hush fell over the underworld, the kind that comes when predators finish feeding. The message was clear. Vito had restored order.

But the man himself was fading.

On December 23, 2013, the Godfather of Montreal, the last real *Capo di tutti i Capi*, Boss of all Bosses, north of the border, died in Sacré Coeur Hospital from complications tied to lung cancer. Just like that, the vendetta ended. The war machine shut down. The eye of the storm passed.

No gunfire. No police raid. Just a hospital bed, a heart monitor, and a dynasty gasping its final breath.

Some in the underworld refused to believe it. Rumors spread poison, radiation exposure, a slow-played hit. But no hard evidence ever surfaced. Doctors signed off on a natural death. Still, those closest to the game knew better. It wasn't just Vito that died. It was the last chance Montreal's Mafia had at true unity.

There was no succession plan. No next in line.

His son was buried. His father was gunned down. His *consigliere* vanished into dust. What remained were fragments. Lieutenants in hiding, loyalists in prison, and a city full of vultures circling what used to be a throne.

For one blood-soaked year, Vito had clawed back control from the abyss. He had reminded Montreal what it meant to move in fear, to speak in whispers, to obey.

And then, just like that, he was gone.

When a king dies without an heir, the vultures feast. Vito Rizzuto's death left a power vacuum the size of Montreal's underworld, and everyone wanted a piece. The streets didn't mourn. They mobilized.

The Rizzuto name still carried fear, but there was no longer a hand on the wheel. The next generation, Leonardo Rizzuto, Vito's surviving son, and Stefano Sollecito, son of old *consigliere* Rocco, tried to steer the remnants. But they weren't Vito. They weren't even close.

They dressed the part. They said the right things. But the sharks could smell it. They weren't killers, not in the old-school sense. They were administrators, not enforcers. In a world where reputation kept you alive, Leonardo and Sollecito were walking targets.

Meanwhile, the Hells Angels were still reeling from SharQc. Their elite Nomads were buried in indictments. Their puppet clubs were fractured. What was left of their power base had gone into survival mode, pivoting to low-profile hustles. Trucking fronts, real estate plays, offshore accounts, construction contracts.

The alliance that once moved dope from port to province, taxed the streets, and controlled the city's heartbeat was dead. In its place was chaos. Deals fell through. Debt collection turned into bloodshed. The criminal map of Montreal, once neatly divided between two giants, became a jigsaw puzzle of micro-empires, shifting alliances, and untrustworthy soldiers.

In April 2014, the hammer dropped. Boucher was expelled from the club. Cut loose. Stripped of his colors. After decades of loyalty, bloodshed, and power, the Angels washed their hands of him. The man who once rode at the front of the pack was now officially excommunicated, a fallen angel in solitary silence.

And into that chaos stepped new blood, young, volatile, and nothing like the old guard. If the old mafia and the old bikers had rules, the street gangs had none. They didn't play chess. They played demolition derby. And in the power vacuum left by the collapse of the Rizzuto dynasty, they moved fast and hit harder.

Crews like the Syndicate, Bo-Gars, and Bloods-affiliated cliques in Montreal North and the West Island didn't wait for permission. They took corners, took customers, took shots often in broad daylight. Most of their members were young, ruthless, and came from neighborhoods where violence wasn't just an occupational hazard, it was a lifestyle.

The new mafia saw opportunity. These gangs were hungry, cheap, and desperate to rise. They didn't ask questions. They just followed orders and collected envelopes.

So, mafia figures started subcontracting them as muscle. Shooters. Collectors. Intimidators. It was cheaper than paying bikers and easier than getting their own hands dirty.

The bikers, meanwhile, didn't trust the street gangs, but they understood the leverage. Some Angels began quietly working with them too, cutting deals for distribution territory or enforcement on the fringes. It was the criminal version of hiring mercenaries, useful but volatile.

And volatility is exactly what followed.

Street gang members didn't operate by the same logic as the bikers or the old mafia. They didn't care about maintaining a reputation through subtlety or hierarchy. They settled debts with bullets, often without warning. They posted selfies with bricks of coke. They filmed themselves with pistols tucked into designer bags. It wasn't just about profit. It was about image, fear, status.

They were uncontrollable.

Drive-bys became more common. Homes were shot up in mistaken identity hits. Innocents got caught in the crossfire. Surveillance footage showed young gang members speeding through downtown in stolen cars, emptying clips into rival hangouts, then disappearing into housing blocks.

This wasn't the underworld anymore. It was spilling into the daylight. Into public parks, shopping centers, suburban strip malls.

The Angels and the new mafia both realized something far too late. The street gangs weren't just muscle. They were a third faction. One that neither side could fully control and both had helped empower. The alliances that had once given each side strength were now giving birth to chaos.

And law enforcement was watching it all unfold in real time.

For years, Montreal's underworld had been a black box, impenetrable, disciplined, and tight-lipped. During the reign of Vito Rizzuto, the walls didn't leak. Phones weren't used. Messages were passed face-to-face, or not at all. No one talked. Everyone knew the consequences.

But this new generation? They were reckless.

They texted threats. They made calls without burners. Some even joked about hits on Instagram. It wasn't just arrogance. It was ignorance. They didn't fear wiretaps because they didn't think like mobsters. They thought like street dealers, fast money, fast moves, no exit plan.

And that's exactly what law enforcement had been waiting for.

The *Sûreté du Québec*, RCMP, and Montreal police began intercepting calls and messages like they were tuning into a criminal radio station. With surveillance already high from the fallout of the biker war and the Rizzuto collapse, all it took was a few slip-ups, and suddenly the picture came into focus.

Operation Magot-Mastiff was born out of this chaos. A wiretap-based dragnet that surveilled bikers, mobsters, and street gangs alike. They bugged bars. Cafés. Clubhouses. Burner phones. Even cars.

And what they heard was gold.

Conversations between bikers and mafiosi where mutual disdain dripped from every sentence. A patch-holder calling his mafia "partner" a "rat-in-waiting." A young mafioso referring to the Angels as "clowns on Harleys." Enforcers talking about extortion jobs. Mid-level dealers warning of rip crews. Arguments about shipments, debts, and snitches, some names spoken out loud, others hinted at in nicknames and slang.

And most importantly, they heard fear.

No one trusted anyone anymore. Soldiers feared their own capos. Bikers second-guessed alliances. Street gangs were playing both sides, then pocketing the fallout. It was a pressure cooker of paranoia.

One recorded call captured a known mob associate venting to a girlfriend about how he couldn't trust his own guys. "They're either gonna kill me or flip on me," he said. "Fuckin' vultures everywhere."

Law enforcement didn't need to break the code. The criminals were doing it for them.

They hit them like a thunderclap.

June 2014. After years of surveillance, wiretaps, and carefully built cases, law enforcement unleashed Operation Clemenza, a surgical strike aimed not just at individuals but at the entire criminal scaffolding propping up Montreal's underworld.

The raids were coordinated, sweeping across the city at dawn. More than 30 suspects were taken down, mobsters, bikers, facilitators, and middlemen. The cops didn't knock. They kicked in doors.

Clemenza was bigger than a bust. It was a statement.

Over 1,400 recorded conversations were submitted as evidence, unfiltered windows into the dysfunction eating both the new mafia and the old bikers alive. It was clear from the transcripts: no one was in control. Deals were falling apart. Territory was being double-sold. Street gangs were reneging on payments. Even within organizations, loyalty was decaying like meat in the sun.

The Rizzuto Family name, once sacred, was barely mentioned in reverence. The bikers were no longer unified. The Nomads had internal rifts, with some chapters quietly doing business behind the backs of others. One Angel was even caught on tape saying, "We're not a brotherhood anymore, we're a fucking vending machine. Whoever puts in gets what they want."

The evidence was damning. Drug transactions. Death threats. Price negotiations on kilos of coke and meth. Schemes to hide weapons. Plans to torch businesses behind on payments. Names of corrupt union officials. Hints of political connections. It was all there. All laid bare.

And once the first domino fell, others followed fast. Some suspects lawyered up. Others ran. A few, under pressure, cracked. By 2015, indictments were stacking up in court like body bags. Prosecutors, using Canada's anti-gang laws, didn't even need to prove individual crimes, just association with a criminal organization.

Convictions came quick. The mob lost key players. The Angels lost lieutenants. Some received double-digit sentences. Others, facing life, chose to cooperate. Testimony from once-loyal soldiers painted a picture of chaos, betrayal, and disintegration. The underworld was hemorrhaging leadership, and nobody was stepping up to stop it.

It wasn't just the arrests that broke them. It was the silence. The kind of silence that creeps in after a betrayal. The kind that settles like a fog inside the heads of men who once ruled the streets and now weren't sure who to trust, or if they'd wake up with a barrel in their mouth. Some fled Montreal altogether. Mid-level mafia operators slipped across the border to Florida or upstate New York. A few patched bikers relocated to the Prairies or went dark in rural Quebec. They didn't run from the police. They ran from each other.

Because the real fear wasn't prison. It was betrayal.

Guys who used to party together, bury bodies together, sit down over steaks and plan half-million-dollar moves now couldn't look each other in the eye. No one knew who had flipped. Who wore a wire. Who gave up the safe house, the stash location, the phone number? Even rumors of cooperation were enough to spark hits.

Law enforcement fed the paranoia. Quiet raids. Strategic leaks. Sudden asset seizures. Names floated in the media unconfirmed, but just believable enough to sow suspicion. It was psychological warfare, and it worked better than bullets.

People stopped showing up to meetings. Phones stopped ringing. Messages were delivered through third-hand whispers, if at all. Whole networks froze, afraid to move a gram or collect a debt. Even the old guard, what was left of it, sensed the walls closing in. Some of the surviving Rizzuto affiliates tried to regroup, but it was like rebuilding a church on scorched earth. Too many ghosts. Too many lies. Too many enemies who used to be friends.

December 1, 2014. Tony Callocchio goes down over lunch. Montreal. Midday. Tony Callocchio sat at a posh suburban bistro, chewing through lunch like it was just another Tuesday. Connected to the old Di Maulo crew, tight with Moreno Gallo. But his past caught up before dessert. A shooter walked in, put bullets in him right at the table. Patrons screamed. Blood on linen.

March 1, 2016. Lorenzo "Skunk" Giordano clipped outside a gym. He was acting underboss, a street-hardened veteran of the Rizzuto clan. Thought he was untouchable. He was wrong. A hail of bullets dropped him in the parking lot of his Laval fitness club. He'd just finished his workout. He never made it to the car.

May 27, 2016. Rocco "Sauce" Sollecito, acting boss, ambushed at a stop sign. Morning traffic. Broad daylight. Sollecito sat behind the wheel of his luxury SUV, less than 100 yards from a police station. A shooter approached like a ninja, squeezed the trigger. One of Montreal's most respected mob elders was gone in a flash of lead and glass.

June 2, 2016. Angelo D'Onofrio, iced with espresso. The old-school mobster sat outside *Café Sinatra*, sipping espresso like it was 1985. No guards. No worry. A man walked up, shot him dead on the spot. The brass shells hit cobblestones, the blood ran through the gutters.

June 30, 2016. Joe and Vinnie Falduto vanish into the ether. Low-level muscle, running errands for bigger names. They disappeared one quiet summer night. No bodies. No ransom. No goodbye. Just gone. Presumed dead, eaten by the game.

October 15, 2016. Vince Spagnolo shot outside his own house. A trusted Rizzuto messenger and advisor. Spagnolo was a survivor, but survival has an expiration date in this world. He made it to his driveway, but not through it. They shot him before he could unlock the door.

March 14, 2017. Mila Barberi, collateral beauty. Toronto. 28 years old. Barberi was sitting in the car of her boyfriend, mob figure Saverio Serrano, when the bullets came. She died in a stranger's war. The killers missed Serrano.

March 18, 2017. Nicola "Big Nicky" Di Marco gunned down. Lieutenant to Ponytail De Vito. Known for his muscle and mouth. Somebody finally shut both.

May 2, 2017. Hamilton's war begins. Angelo "Big Ange" Musitano took two to the head in his own driveway. The Musitano name had weight, but bullets weigh more.

August 17, 2017. Antonio De Blasio killed outside football practice. One of Sauce Sollecito's best friends. His kid was on the field when the shots rang out.

November 2, 2017. Jacques Desjardins disappears. Brother of Raynald. Quiet. Calculating. Gone. No witnesses. No body. Just another ghost in the fog of war.

February 3, 2018. Daniel "Dark Danny" Ranieri found dead in Mexico. Rizzuto family's Ontario crew boss. Vanished for two years dodging indictments. They caught up in Mexico. No warning. Just blood.

June 28, 2018. Steve "Stevie the Jew" Ovadia clipped at a strip mall. He was flashy, cocky, and marked. When it came, it came quick, bullets in the parking lot, no mask, no mercy.

June 29, 2018. Cosimo "Little C" Commisso and his girlfriend killed. Nephew of Cosimo "The Quail" Commisso, Ontario mob boss. Gunned down, both of them. No survivors. No forgiveness.

September 13, 2018. Al Ivarone taken out in Scenic Woods. Hamilton enforcer. Paid the price for gambling territory beefs in Niagara Falls and ties to the Angelo Musitano hit. Shot dead at his home.

January 24, 2019. Tony "The Builder" Magi gets built into the pavement. Construction mogul. Connected. Targeted for years and was suspected of possibly being the setup man in the "Ritzy Nick" Rizzuto hit. He finally got caught on a construction site. Dead before his workers knew what hit him.

January 30, 2019. CeCe Luppino killed in his parents' driveway. The 43-year-old's dad, Rocco, is a heavyweight in the Hamilton mafia scene, as was his grandfather Giacomo. The Luppino name had weight. Not enough. The bullets didn't care.

February 14, 2019. Ray Khano dead in the street. Drug pusher. Linked to Rizzuto crime family leader "Compare Frank" Arcadi. Caught slipping in the Montreal suburbs. Forty-three years old. One final deal too many.

March 25, 2019. Mike Di Battista gunned down in the Dominican Republic. Mob enforcer. Tied to Liborio "Poncho" Cuntrera. Shot behind the wheel. Caribbean sun, Canadian blood.

March 29, 2019. Mario Simeone gets smoked. Another Tony Magi affiliate. Another name crossed off in the silent ledger.

May 4, 2019. Salvatore Scoppa assassinated in a crowded hotel lobby. One-time ally turned traitor. Montreal. Crowded hotel. One bullet ended a long betrayal.

August 16, 2019. Paulo Caputo dies in front of his restaurant on Roncesvalles Avenue. Toronto. Daylight. Customers inside. A massacre in front of the meatballs.

October 21, 2019. Andrew Scoppa joins his brother in hell. The West End of Montreal. A strip mall parking lot. Two in the chest. One in the head.

November 7, 2019. Antonio "Scratchy" Fiorda murdered outside a shopping mall. Enforcer. Loyal to the Commiso clan. It didn't matter. He bled like everyone else.

March 5, 2020. George Barresi down in Hamilton. Bookie. Real estate guy. Made the wrong bet.

July 10, 2020. Pasquale "Fat Pat" Musitano blown away in broad daylight. Parking lot in Burlington. Shot to pieces. Years of grudges settled in seconds.

The Angels, while still formidable, had lost their grip. Without the mafia as partners, they had to shoulder more risk themselves. They began sourcing coke directly from South

American cartels, cutting out the middlemen and exposing themselves in the process. Some chapters grew bold. Others splintered off. The structure that had once been a fortress was showing cracks.

And the street gangs?

They kept rising. They had no hierarchy to collapse. No past to protect. No myths to uphold. They were cheaper, younger, faster, and they didn't care who used to run Montreal. They only cared about who controlled it now.

And the alliance between the Rizzuto mafia and the Hells Angels didn't explode. It rotted.

It died not with a bang, but with a slow, brutal erosion of trust, discipline, and fear. What was once a billion-dollar criminal empire built on order and respect became a fractured battlefield ruled by ego, greed, and paranoia.

Law enforcement didn't topple it alone. The players destroyed themselves one body, one betrayal, one wiretap at a time. And in the end, all that was left were ghosts. Court transcripts. Seized bank accounts. Surveillance tapes. Dead men in ditches. Silent phones. And a city where the underworld still moves, but never again like it did under Vito.

With the Mafia in disarray and the Angels wounded, the streets belonged to the wolves now.

Haitian and Arab street gangs, once treated as pawns or subcontractors, rose like fire through the cracks. Crews like Bo-Gars, Syndicate, and Blood Family Mafia weren't interested in tradition. They didn't care about *omertà*, patches, or loyalty to dead dons. They cared about product, power, and paper.

They had learned from the giants how to flood neighborhoods with crack and fentanyl, how to enforce through fear, how to move like ghosts in the night. But they added something new. Raw aggression and zero accountability. They weren't afraid of the bikers. They weren't intimidated by the name Rizzuto. They shot first, posted about it later, and brought a level of volatility that neither the Mafia nor the Angels were built to handle.

These weren't negotiations. These were takeovers.

They carved up corners, seized networks, and taxed anything that moved. And when the old guard tried to push back, they responded with war gunfire outside nightclubs, home invasions in Laval, dealers executed in stairwells. They didn't ask permission. They took.

Some older mobsters tried to align with the new players. A few even subcontracted street crews to do collections and hits. But the balance of power had shifted. The streets didn't answer to the Mafia anymore. Montreal's criminal world belonged to the young, the ruthless, and the leaderless. And that made it more dangerous than ever.

By 2015, the war that had scorched Montreal's underworld for a decade didn't end. It simply ran out of blood. There was no treaty. No handshake in a dimly lit café. Just exhaustion. Fear. Survival instinct.

The Mafia, under new leadership, tried to project strength. But the truth was clear. They were holding together a name, not an empire. The old hierarchy was gone. The soldiers were fractured. Many were in prison or six feet under. What remained was branding without firepower.

The Hells Angels, still rebuilding after SharQc, took a different path. They moved quieter, dirtier, and deeper. The flash was gone, replaced by front companies, fake contracts, and buried cash. Strip clubs became business hubs.

Construction projects masked trafficking. A new generation of bikers wore suits instead of cuts, and profits flowed, but the dominance was diluted.

And in the middle of this uneasy balance stood the street gangs, holding more turf than ever before. They didn't run Montreal, but they ran parts of it, and no one could ignore them.

Police pressure didn't let up either. Operations like *Clemenza*, *Magma*, and *Loquace* kept the heat on every faction, seizing encrypted phones, freezing accounts, flipping soldiers. Every move was watched. Every alliance wiretapped. Every misstep punished.

What emerged from the ashes wasn't a new empire. It was a criminal patchwork.

The Mafia still had prestige, but not power.

The Hells Angels had infrastructure, but less reach.

The street gangs had firepower, but no structure.

And the port Montreal's golden goose was now contested, fractured, and swarming with watchers.

The golden age of underworld order was gone.

What remained was a fragile peace not out of respect, but necessity. Everyone knew the cost of open war now. It wasn't just bullets. It was surveillance, betrayal, headlines, and prison time.

And yet beneath it all, the grudges still burned. The ghosts of Vito, Mom, Nicolo, Nick Jr., and dozens of others still haunted the alleys and backrooms. The alliances were dead, but the memories weren't.

The giants had fallen. The kings were gone. But the game? The game never ended.

# Part V: Legacy

# Chapter 13

# What Remains

By the end of the 2010s, Montreal's underworld looked like a battlefield long after the fighting had stopped, scarred, silent, but far from abandoned.

The giants had fallen. The Rizzuto dynasty was fractured. The Hells Angels were regrouping. What remained wasn't a throne, but a graveyard of reputations, and a handful of men trying to walk through the ashes without choking on the smoke.

Leonardo walked quietly. The surviving son of Vito Rizzuto, he was a lawyer by training and, at least on paper, clean. He didn't carry his father's swagger or his grandfather's Sicilian fire, but his name was heavy enough to turn heads and to land him in court.

In 2015, he was arrested during Project *Magot-Mastiff*, alongside none other than Stefano Sollecito, son of the late *consigliere* Rocco Sollecito. The symbolism was too loud to ignore. A Rizzuto and a Sollecito once again tied to power, shadow, and the remains of the old alliance.

And the Hells Angels? Right there in the room, arms-length. The charges wouldn't stick. A judge threw out key wiretap evidence on a technicality. But even if the law walked away, the message was clear. They were still in the game. Only now, it was a different game entirely.

Other names surfaced, flickering briefly before being wiped off the board. Francesco Del Balso, once a trusted lieutenant of Vito, gunned down in 2023. Lorenzo Giordano, murdered in Laval after stepping back into the mix. Raynald Desjardins, mastermind turned pariah, rotting in prison for a hit gone wrong. The Rizzuto name wasn't dead, but it no longer ruled. It haunted.

The Hells Angels don't die. They hibernate. They rebuild.

After the hammer of Operation SharQc came down in 2009, the club looked finished: 156 arrests, multiple murders pinned to their patch, and a public image battered beyond repair. But by the late 2010s, they were back. Not loud. Not proud. But back. This time, they learned from their wounds.

No more parking Harleys outside strip clubs for the press to snap. No more open-air intimidation. Instead, quiet money. Commercial fronts. Trucks. Real estate. Crypto.

Martin Robert became the name to watch, a seasoned player with influence across chapters in Quebec and beyond. Word on the street was that Robert moved more like a CFO than a warlord. He knew the new rules. Keep your head down, keep your people paid, and let someone else take the fall if it goes sideways.

They expanded east to New Brunswick, Ontario, Northern Quebec. Places with less heat, more opportunity. The Angels were never about tradition. They were about adaptation. And in this new criminal economy, discretion was the new leather jacket. Into the void stepped a different breed, young, hungry, and without reverence. They didn't quote old codes. They didn't know who Nicolo Rizzuto was, or care. They wore balaclavas, not gold chains. Their wars played out in public housing stairwells and Instagram stories, not five-star bistros in Little Italy.

Haitian gangs like Bo-Gars, Syndicate Montreal, and Blood Family Mafia controlled crack and fentanyl pipelines. Arab crews from North and East Montreal handled cyber scams, weapons, and cartel links. Indigenous networks held key corridors along the U.S. border at Akwesasne, unguarded land that moved guns and people with silent ease. These weren't organizations. They were ecosystems. Loose. Ruthless. Wildly effective.

A kilo of coke still moved through the Port of Montreal, but now it was harder to track, harder to tax. Nobody asked permission anymore. If you could move product, you had power. And if you couldn't protect your turf, you were out. Permanently. The new players didn't want to inherit the kingdom. They wanted to burn it down and build something else faster, bloodier, and smarter.

What remained from the war years wasn't just new factions and dead names. It was a hard-earned list of truths, paid for in bodies.

*Loyalty Is a Lie.* The myth of *omertà* died when Vito's own circle betrayed him. When Paolo Renda vanished. When internal beefs spilled into the open. In the end, everyone was expendable if the money was right.

*Flash Brings Fire.* The Rizzutos held court in fine restaurants. The Angels paraded in public. The next generation learned better. They stayed off the radar, hid behind shell companies and fake names. They saw what happened when you flew too close to the limelight.

*Business Is the Only Code.* The old world talked about respect. The new world talks about margins. Violence still exists, but now, it's strategic, not theatrical. A rival disappears only if it affects the bottom line.

*The Game Evolves or Dies.* The Mafia became brokers. The Angels became wholesalers. The gangs became retailers. Cartels, meanwhile, watched it all and adjusted. Nobody owns Montreal now, but everybody uses it.

Montreal's underworld used to be a machine. Smooth, layered, hierarchical. Today, it's a mosaic, a fragmented sprawl of factions, alliances, and backroom deals.

One corner might be run by a Haitian crew paying tribute to a biker wholesaler. Another by an Arab syndicate leasing smuggling routes from an old Rizzuto cousin. A third by a 22-year-old kid with crypto wallets and cartel product. Nobody rules everything. But everybody rules something.

The Rizzutos exist in whispers. *Les Hells* exist in paperwork. The new players exist everywhere, seen but rarely understood. The final truth is that there was never really honor among thieves. The alliance between the Rizzutos and the Angels was built not on respect, but on utility. It was profit over protocol. And when the risks outweighed the rewards, the knives came out. Quietly. Then loudly.

In betrayal, they collapsed. In alliance, they flourished. In legacy, they left a map and a warning.

And now?

The old guard is gone. The kids are running the streets. The game has no king.

But the rules?

The rules still bleed.

By the 2020s, Montreal is still a criminal city, but it's no longer an empire. It's a network. A grid of silent meetings, encrypted chats, fake shell companies, and blurred allegiances. The names have changed. The weapons have evolved. The fear still lingers. And every time a body drops on Saint-Michel or a kilo vanishes at the port, the shadows whisper the same truth.

The kings are gone.

But the game?

The game goes on.

## Chapter 14

## Headlines and Blood-Soaked Narratives

The public's view of Montreal's underworld was shaped as much by journalists as it was by police. From the Montreal Gazette to Radio-Canada, the media walked a precarious line covering crime without becoming its next target. Still, in the wake of high-profile assassinations and mass arrests, headlines turned bold.

"*The Godfather Falls*,"
"*Mob Crackdown Rocks Montreal*,"
"*End of les Hells?*"

The murder of Nicolo Rizzuto, captured by surveillance camera, played on national news for days. It was more than a killing. It was a symbol. A man once regarded as Montreal's "*Capo di Tutti Capi*" had been taken out on his own turf, by his own people, or so many believed.

Likewise, images of leather-clad Hells Angels being marched into court in shackles served as public spectacle and propaganda symbols that no one, not even the most feared men in Canada, were beyond the law.

Yet, the media also contributed to the myth-making. Vito was dubbed the "Teflon Don of the North," a nod to New York's John Gotti. His sharp suits, calm demeanor, and strategic diplomacy made him more than a gangster. He became a character in the public consciousness.

So too, with Mom Boucher, the menacing, muscular ex-prison guard who rose to lead the Hells Angels in Quebec. Boucher was often framed as a ruthless warlord, a man whose ambition knew no bounds, especially after the murders of prison guards in the late '90s.

Documentaries and fictionalized series only cemented these figures into legend. The line between history and drama blurred, and for many outside the chaos, the mafia and bikers became part of the city's identity, dangerous, yes, but also fascinating. But this glamorization carried consequences. It sometimes drew attention away from victims those extorted, beaten, or killed in the shadows. And it fed the next generation of street-level criminals who saw not cautionary tales, but role models.

As bodies piled up in Montreal's alleyways, driveways, and cafes, the violence that once simmered in the shadows exploded into the public consciousness. It wasn't just a criminal feud. It became a spectacle. The media seized upon the underworld conflict between the Rizzutos and the Angels with a mix of breathless fascination and moral panic, transforming assassins into anti-heroes, and turf wars into serialized tragedy.

From the late 1990s into the 2010s, newspapers like *Le Journal de Montréal*, *La Presse*, and *The Montreal Gazette* ran front-page stories with graphic details, surveillance photos, and court sketch artistry that bordered on noir fiction. Headlines screamed of *"The Godfather of Canada"* or *"Angels of Death,"* dramatizing every twist in the criminal saga. Every murder scene drew camera crews. Every police raid was filmed from helicopters.

The killings of Renda and Nicolo in particular became flashpoints for media sensationalism. Photographs of Nicolo's body slumped in his own kitchen, gold chains glinting in the flash of police cameras, became a symbol of the empire's crumbling facade. Local media didn't just report it created narrative arcs, framing Vito as a fallen king returning from exile, hell-bent on vengeance.

While the Hells Angels were often portrayed as brutish thugs leather-clad, tattooed, and crude, the Rizzutos were framed with a surprising romanticism. Vito, in particular, was often painted as a "Gentleman Don," a sharp-suited, diplomatic, even charismatic figure who abhorred unnecessary violence and operated with a sense of order and rules.

This image was not entirely inaccurate, but it was curated, shaped both by myth and by Vito's own efforts to appear reasonable in contrast to the chaos his absence unleashed. Media interviews with lawyers, former detectives, and even mob family acquaintances reinforced the idea that Vito's reign, though criminal, brought "stability."

Documentaries and television specials echoed this theme. French-language programs like *JE* and English ones like CBC's *Fifth Estate* or *W5* chronicled the biker wars and Mafia feuds with dramatic reenactments and music, emphasizing the power struggle and underworld politics like a modern-day *Game of Thrones*.

The public devoured these stories. Ratings spiked, comment sections flooded, and books flew off shelves. This wasn't just news. It was crime as entertainment. The average Montrealer, sipping coffee in a Mile End café, could now name half a dozen mobsters and bikers the way they'd name hockey players.

But media attention came with consequences. Sensationalism put pressure on law enforcement to act swiftly, sometimes prematurely. It also elevated certain underworld figures, making them more famous and therefore more dangerous or more targeted. Internal paranoia deepened. Everyone assumed they were being watched or recorded, because often they were.

In retrospect, the media's framing of the war was both a blessing and a curse. It exposed corruption and forced transparency, but it also created mythology. The Rizzutos weren't Robin Hoods, and the Hells Angels weren't simply misunderstood rebels. Beneath the headlines were blood-soaked vendettas, extortion, addiction, and ruined lives.

Still, for better or worse, the narrative stuck. The war between the Rizzuto Family and the Hells Angels became part of Montreal's modern folklore, etched not just in police files, but in popular imagination.

Long after the blood dried and courtrooms emptied, the legends of the Rizzutos and the Hells Angels endured not just as criminal organizations but as mythological figures in the Canadian psyche. Their names carried weight not only in law enforcement dossiers but in barroom conversations, crime documentaries, and whispered street lore. In a city like Montreal, where power, style, and shadow dance in close proximity, these syndicates became more than crime groups. They became symbols.

The Rizzuto Family, especially under Vito's reign, was seen as a Canadian version of the Sicilian mafia elite. Polished, diplomatic, multilingual, and deeply connected, they embodied a kind of criminal sophistication that stood in stark contrast to the brutish image of traditional mobsters.

The mythos of the Rizzutos was built on several pillars. Discretion, legacy, and influence. Nicolo's migration from Sicily to Canada and his slow, strategic takeover of the Cotroni family empire gave the family a near-royal status in Montreal's criminal underworld. Vito's leadership only added polish. He was educated, refined, and shrewd, dealing not just in drugs and money but in relationships.

Media coverage and court testimony revealed a man who preferred negotiation to violence, who brokered peace between warring factions and could walk through both corporate boardrooms and mob hangouts with equal comfort. His imprisonment, return, and vengeful campaign only added to the myth. The fallen king who reclaimed his throne, if only for a moment.

Even in death, Vito's legend persisted. Some saw him as the last true godfather in North America, an operator of the old code in a modern world spinning into chaos. His name continues to echo in books, documentaries, and criminal folklore as the man who once held Montreal's underworld together by force of respect alone.

In contrast to the Rizzutos' Sicilian poise, the Hells Angels carved their legend through spectacle and domination. Their myth was one of raw power of territory claimed through force, and reputations forged in fire. They weren't born of immigrant struggle or mafia tradition but of rebellion, postwar disillusionment, and biker brotherhood.

Yet the Canadian chapter of the Hells Angels, especially the Quebec wing, defied stereotypes. Under leaders like Mom Boucher, *Les Hells* evolved from ragtag misfits to a disciplined, multi-million-dollar criminal enterprise. They ran drugs, controlled prostitution rings, and maintained an iron grip on the streets, enforcing loyalty with fear and precision.

Their patch, the iconic Death Head, became a brand that inspired awe and terror alike. Even law-abiding citizens knew not to speak their name lightly. That silence, enforced through fire bombings, beatings, and the occasional public assassination, only deepened their aura.

Like the Rizzutos, the Angels carefully curated their image. The outlaw as a businessman, the gang as a corporation. Their clubhouse wasn't just a hangout. It was a fortress. Their annual rides weren't just social. They were shows of force. They made sure the public remembered that even if the mafia wore suits, the Angels had the muscle.

Together, the Rizzuto Family and the Hells Angels formed a strange mythology, one rooted in alliance and torn apart by betrayal. Their years of cooperation were seen by some as a golden age of underworld order, while others viewed it as a dark pact that allowed violence to be outsourced and crimes to scale. When the alliance frayed, the myths only grew.

Was it greed or pride that caused the break? Did old-school values collapse under the weight of modern chaos? Theories abound. What remains undeniable is this. Their story is no longer just criminal history. It's cultural memory. Like Al Capone or Pablo Escobar, Vito and Mom are now characters in the broader narrative of crime and consequence. Their names live on in news archives, true crime novels, court transcripts, and whispered warnings. Whether as villains, legends, or relics of a bygone era, their mythos persists, and the city they once ruled has never been the same.

Law, order, and *omertà* each played its part in shaping the rise and fall of Canada's greatest criminal empire. In the end, the silence was broken, the law prevailed in courtrooms, and the stories once hidden in shadows became part of the country's enduring true crime canon.

# Chapter 15

# The Reluctant Prince

When Vito died of natural causes in December 2013, it wasn't just the passing of a man. It was the death knell of an era. The old boss, the peacemaker, the architect of Montreal's underworld alliance, was gone. And with him went the last true sense of order. What remained was uncertainty and the creeping scent of blood in the air.

By 2015, the streets of Montreal were soaked in blood and whispers. The old guard had been burned down, buried, or vanished. The Rizzuto dynasty, a name once uttered in backrooms with reverence or fear, had been gutted from the inside out. Vito was gone. His father, his son, his inner circle gone. What was left was a smoldering empire without a king.

And into that vacuum stepped a man who never wanted the throne.

Leonardo Rizzuto.

Leonardo wasn't your typical mobster. He was polished, reserved. A man of the courtroom, not the corner. He wore tailored suits instead of tracksuits, carried a law degree instead of a gun. For most of his adult life, he stayed in the legitimate world, playing by the rules in a city built on bending them. He had the name, but he never flaunted it.

But bloodlines are destiny in the underworld, and legacy doesn't ask your permission.

By the mid-2010s, law enforcement began watching him closely. The RCMP and Montreal police tagged him as one half of a new power duo rising from the ashes. Leonardo Rizzuto and Stefano Sollecito.

Young blood. New suits. Same name. Same weight.

They weren't the street-brawling bosses of the old world. These guys moved different, quieter, cleaner, but no less dangerous. They stepped onto a chessboard littered with corpses and broken codes, where every move was life or death. If Vito had ruled with iron charm and Sicilian cunning, Leonardo was the cold tactician, the Canadian Michael Corleone.

He hadn't just inherited a name. He inherited a war.

Over fifteen years, the Montreal Mafia war tore through the city like a wildfire with no windbreak. RCMP intelligence estimates placed the body count in the triple digits, stretching across provinces, countries, and oceans. The Sicilians, the Calabrians, the bikers, the street gangs, everyone had skin in the game, and everyone had scores to settle. The battlefield had no borders.

The rules? Gone.

Leonardo wasn't built to be a gangster. But by the time the smoke started clearing, he was wearing the crown.

These weren't old-school dons. They were second-generation mobsters, born into privilege and expectation, now presiding over a broken kingdom. The streets had changed. The old enforcers were either six feet under or rotting in federal cells. Rivals had grown bold. Street gangs no longer bowed their heads. And the bikers, well, the bikers were evolving too.

For a brief moment, Leonardo and Stefano tried to play kingmakers. They cut deals with Calabrian mobsters, negotiated with remnants of the Hells Angels, and tried to bring unity to a syndicate splintered by years of bloodshed. They were quiet operators, more boardroom than back alley, but the rules had changed. No one feared the Rizzutos like they once did.

Then, the police came knocking.

Operation Magot-Mastiff hit like a wrecking ball in late 2015. Wiretaps, surveillance, café bugs, dozens arrested, including Leonardo and Stefano. The charges ranged from drug trafficking to gangsterism. Conversations that once whispered across espresso cups were now played back in courtrooms.

Though Leonardo would walk free in 2018, the verdict didn't wipe the slate clean. It just painted a bigger target on his back. His name was back in circulation, not as the untouchable prince of Montreal, but as prey.

Meanwhile, July 10, 2022, marked the quiet death of a giant. Mom Boucher, the outlaw king who once made the streets kneel, died in palliative care, shackled not by cuffs, but by cancer. Throat cancer. A poetic curse for a man whose voice once ordered the living into graves. He was 69. No goddamn roaring Harleys. No fucking last ride. No biker salute. Just a big middle finger, a sterile room, the hum of machines, and a legacy soaked in blood.

The empire he had bled for had already buried him in spirit. The streets he ruled barely remembered his name. The brothers he commanded had left him to rot. No blaze of glory, just a slow fade into irrelevance. End of the road.

But the war didn't die with him.

March 16, 2023. Laval. Just after noon. The sky was clear, the road wide open. Leonardo sat low in the driver's seat of his black Mercedes, the hum of the engine under him, one hand resting lightly on the wheel. Highway 440 stretched ahead like a ribbon of asphalt calm.

Then, like a crack of thunder, hell opened up. Then came the wolves.

Two cars slid into position, predators circling their mark. Matching late-model Porsche sports cars, one black, one blood-red. No hesitation. No warning. Just a staccato roar as muzzles flashed.

The windshield erupted. Glass sprayed like shrapnel. The air inside turned into a storm of lead and smoke. Bullets chewed through the metal skin of the Mercedes, punched into the leather seats, and sparked off the dashboard.

One round found him, hot steel tearing into his leg. The wheel jerked in his hands. Tires screamed. The world tilted into chaos.

But Leonardo didn't fold. He kept the car alive, forcing it forward, blood soaking into his pants, heart hammering like a war drum. In the rearview, the Porsches peeled off, their job unfinished.

By the time the smoke cleared, Leonardo was still breathing, but the message was carved deep. Being Vito's son wouldn't save you anymore. The game had changed, and the hunters wore new colors.

The attack didn't just rattle glass. It rattled the city.

Within hours, the RCMP rolled into Laval heavy. Unmarked SUVs. Command truck. Temporary ops center set up like they were hunting a terrorist cell. The official line was "public safety," but everyone on the street knew they were circling around the Rizzuto name.

Word spread fast through Montreal's underworld. The shooters weren't freelancers. They were playing for a crew with reach, power, and enough muscle to hit a boss in broad daylight. The chatter pointed one way, toward the Hells Angels, and a faction inside hungry to finish what the coup years earlier had started.

The whispers had names.

Francesco "Chit" Del Balso. Once Vito's boy, a driver, sometimes a bodyguard, a man who could be charming in one breath and promise to break you in half the next. He'd done time with Rizzuto heavyweights, kept his ear to both the Sicilian and biker sides, and lately, word was, he'd hitched his wagon to Marty "The *Capo*" Robert, the Montreal HA boss with a Canada-sized plan.

If Del Balso was in on the March hit, he'd missed. And in this game, missing the king doesn't buy you more time. It buys you a death sentence.

That balance was already splintering. The old pact between the Sicilians and the bikers, the alliance that had run drugs, guns, and money for decades, was in pieces. Now it was a street war in slow motion, every move measured but deadly.

The March ambush should have been the end of Leonardo. Instead, it became the beginning of something worse. The day after the hit, the city's underworld moved like a shaken hornet's nest. Crews circled wagons. Side alleys hummed with lookouts. Little Italy was locked down so tight you couldn't sneeze without someone clocking you. New alliances were whispered into being, street gangs in Quebec City, former enemies turned mercenaries, anyone willing to bleed for the cause.

June 5, 2023. Dorval, West Island. Midday. Monster Gym. Del Balso had a routine workout, shook hands, and showed the neighborhood he was untouchable. He pulled out of the lot like he owned the pavement.

He didn't make it to the street.

A gunman stepped in close. No warning. No talk. Just metal barking over and over until Del Balso slumped behind the wheel, blood blooming down his shirt. The hitman vanished before the echoes died, gone into the heat shimmer like he'd never been there.

Boom. Done. Just like that. It was clean. Cold. Surgical. Exactly the kind of hit you lay down when you want to erase a problem, not make a scene.

By nightfall, the cops had a new theory. Maybe it wasn't just a vendetta. Maybe the Hells Angels themselves greenlit the whole thing. Not to protect Del Balso, but to clean up his mess.

Del Balso had sat down with the Angels' brass right before he got clipped. Word drifting up from the U.S. biker hierarchy was clear. They didn't like how the failed hit on Leonardo Rizzuto made them look. Bad optics. In this world, loyalty isn't just currency. It's survival. And the bosses didn't want anything that could rattle their alliances with the Sicilians, the Calabrians, or any of the other Cosa Nostra families tied into the pipeline from Montreal to New York, to Sicily, to South America.

So, as the informant's story goes, *Les Hells* told their Montreal crew to "make things right." And if that meant cutting loose one of their own, so be it. Allegedly, it was Marty Robert who called Del Balso out to that West Island gym. A meeting, a handshake, maybe even a workout. Instead, it was his last ride.

Marty, of course, denies everything. He even showed up at Del Balso's wake, stood by the casket like he was paying respect. That's the biker code. Never admit. Never flinch. Never let the mask slip.

For Leonardo, it was a rare gift in this life, a win he didn't have to fire a shot for. But it wasn't peace. It was just one less wolf at the door.

Because in Montreal, when one enemy drops, another steps into his place.

Del Balso's body wasn't cold before the vultures started circling. His death didn't bring calm. It didn't even slow the war. It just shifted the balance for a minute, like sand sliding in a glass before the clock started again. In the backrooms and biker clubhouses, in Little Italy's espresso bars and outlaw roadhouses, every player was calculating the same thing. Who's next? Who's taking the shot?

August 18, 2023. Robert "Teflon Rob" Barletta knew what it meant to live with a target on his back. Enemies on both sides of the law, bullets in the shadows, subpoenas in the daylight. He'd been dodging them for years.

This week, he survived his third arson attack, flames licking at his home while tensions between the Hells Angels and the Italian Mafia in Quebec threatened to boil over. But fire was the least of his problems.

Sources say "Teflon Rob," along with his close ally Marty Robert, is under RCMP investigation for possible ties to the June 5th murder of mobster Francesco "Chit" Del Balso. Another body in a war where alliances are paper-thin and payback never sleeps.

November 17, 2023. Greg "Picasso" Woolley had played both sides of Montreal's underworld. An ally to the Rizzuto mob, a trusted partner of the Angels, and the undisputed Godfather of Quebec's street gangs. But even kings fall.

That afternoon, Woolley stepped out of his Lamborghini SUV in the parking lot of a suburban medical center. Moments later, he was gunned down. The shooter? His own protégé and successor, Atna "2Pac" Onha. Sources say Onha pulled the trigger on contract for the Hells Angels.

Word on the street was that Marty and his brass believed Woolley was getting too close to the Rizzutos, ready to swing his muscle back to the Sicilians in the middle of their feud. The Angels couldn't risk it. Better to cut him out before he flipped sides.

Onha offered Marty a sweeter deal than Woolley ever had, more money, more control, a reshuffling of the rackets. The problem? Not everyone wanted to fall in line. That's why Woolley's death was more than a hit. It was the *coup de grâce*.

The move that cemented Robert and Onha's power, at least for now.

November 27, 2023. Quebec City. Michel "Dooney" Guerin was just another man shoveling snow from his driveway. But in the underworld, he was more than that. He was the Angels' taxman in Quebec City, the guy who made sure every gang pushing dope kicked up their cut.

Guerin had history. He once ran The Mercenaries MC, a Hells Angels support club that kept order in the streets and muscle in the bars. Now he was the collector, the enforcer with a smile and a ledger.

That morning in Charlesbourg, he never saw it coming. A burst of gunfire cut him down where he stood, snow stained red in the cold. Another outlaw with ties to the Angels, gone. Another reminder that in Quebec, even the ones holding the books and calling in debts can end up face-down in the driveway.

December 14, 2023. Cancun. Late afternoon heat clung to the air inside the Total Sports gym. Samy "The Shoe" Tamauro was mid-workout, breathing heavy under the fluorescent lights, sweat dripping onto the mat.

The shooter came in silent. No warning. No drama. One step behind him, then one round to the back of the head. Clean. Execution-style. "The Shoe" dropped instantly, face-first, dead before the blood even hit the floor.

The triggerman didn't stick around to see if the job was done. He was already swinging onto the back of a waiting motorcycle, the engine screaming as the bike disappeared into traffic.

Word hit Montreal within hours. Everyone knew it wasn't random. Samy had history. His cousin, Freddy Silva, had been a Rizzuto-connected hit man before flipping in the summer of 2022 in a deal so wild the cops helicoptered him out of prison. When Silva turned rat, people who'd ever shared a table with him started getting nervous. Samy included.

If he'd been hiding out in Mexico, he'd picked the wrong place. That country's become the unofficial exile camp for Quebec gangland figures looking to dodge bullets at home. But the bullets travel now. No one is untouchable.

Samy's death was more than a message. It was proof. This war had no borders. Canada, the United States, and Mexico, it was all one battleground. And if you were marked, they'd find you whether you were in Montreal's East End or under the Caribbean sun.

The war didn't slow down when the calendar in the New Year. If anything, it got bloodier.

Ali "Ice Cube" Chaaban, Onha's car-theft lieutenant, dodged death twice, once in a drive-by that tore into his arm, and again when gunmen lit up his restaurant. The streets were hunting him.

Then the Woolley crew took a harder hit. Jean-Brandon "Lil' JB" Celestin, Woolley's hand-picked protégé and his "nephew" in everything but blood, was dropped near the crew's Little Italy base. His murder lit a fuse under his older brother, Jean-Phillip "The Butcher" Celestin, Woolley's former enforcer and the boss of the crew. The Butcher wasn't the type to let grief cool into silence.

Just days after Lil' JB's body hit the pavement, the Blood Family Mafia made their move. They tried to snatch veteran Hells Angel Mario "The Banana" Auger. They missed, but days later, they grabbed two of his cousins instead. What followed was pure medieval. One cousin came back missing fingers and toes. The other fought back, killing one of his captors in the struggle.

Retaliation was instant. Within hours, two Red Devils MC members, biker foot soldiers tied to the Angels, were stabbed behind prison walls.

While the Rizzutos were trying to hold the crumbling castle, the Angels were rewriting the playbook.

After Operation SharQc left over 150 bikers and associates behind bars, the Quebec biker world was gutted. The once-feared Mom Boucher was dead. The Laval and Sherbrooke chapters, once powerful, were shadows of themselves.

But death, like power, creates opportunity.

New biker factions were rising in Trois-Rivières, South Shore, and Laval. They were leaner, smarter, and more disciplined. No more bloody turf wars for headlines. These new bikers weren't interested in war. They were interested in profit.

Puppet clubs like the Red Devils, Devil's Ghosts, and Minotaures became their proxies. These were the enforcers, the street-level dealers, the muscle. The full-patch Hells Angels stayed behind the scenes, pulling strings while diversifying into construction, cryptocurrency, and crypto casinos.

They weren't just surviving, they were expanding.

These weren't your grandfather's bikers. They weren't just running meth from a warehouse outside Sherbrooke. They were global now.

In Europe, especially in the Netherlands, Germany, and Scandinavia, Canadian Angels coordinated drug shipments through Rotterdam and Antwerp, smuggling South American cocaine in containers of seafood, machinery, even baby formula. The Port of Montreal became the Canadian hub, a prized entry point for global trafficking.

In Southeast Asia, the Canadians worked with Australian chapters to move precursors for meth. Thai and Filipino contacts provided synthetic drug components. In return, the Canadians gained access to cheap weapons and obscure shipping routes.

From Halifax to Hamburg, from Montreal to Manila, the Hells Angels were becoming a multinational criminal corporation fluent in encrypted messaging, logistics, and transnational laundering.

While Montreal remained symbolic ground, the real turf wars had shifted.

In Southern Ontario, cities like Hamilton, Brantford, and Niagara Falls became battlegrounds. Fentanyl, cocaine, meth shipped in bulk and distributed through puppet clubs. The Outlaws MC fought for control, igniting clashes, clubhouse fires, and bodies in rivers.

Vancouver became something else entirely. A syndicate city. Bikers teamed up with Indo-Canadian and Chinese Triad gangs, dominating real estate, casino laundering, and fentanyl imports from China. These weren't leather-clad warriors. They were men in suits with shell companies and stock portfolios.

Out east, in the Maritimes, the Bacchus MC grew aggressive, challenging Hells Angels' influence in Nova Scotia and New Brunswick, especially at critical ports.

The game was no longer about fear. It was about networks.

In the 2020s, the streets of Montreal hum with the sound of uneasy truces.

The mafia-biker alliance? It still exists, sort of. But it's not a brotherhood anymore. It's business.

And in the shadows of the old order, two new kings were rising.

On one side. Marty "The *Capo*" Robert. Montreal Hells Angels boss. Forty-nine years old, built like a prison weight bench, running his club with the precision of a military campaign.

On the other side. Leonardo "Leo the Lawyer" Rizzuto. Fifty-four years old, the last son of the Rizzuto dynasty still breathing. He'd spent half his life trying to avoid his family's shadow, but by now, there was no escape. His empire had been gutted, key lieutenants dead, alliances shattered, but he wasn't ready to hand it over. Not to Marty. Not to anyone.

Leonardo wore suits, not cuts. A polished lawyer with a law degree, he never had his father's easy way with the Hells Angels. To the bikers, he came off arrogant, like he looked down on them. To Leonardo, the feeling was mutual. He hated being around them, hated the leather, the swagger, the chaos.

"Leonardo was never going to see eye to eye with the Hells Angels," one source said. "The resentment built year after year. Neither side respected the other. This ending wasn't hard to predict if you looked at how the relationship started."

Back in '97, Leo was still a mob prince when he got jumped in a bar by Hells Angels enforcer Donnie "Bam Bam" Magnussen. The bikers left him beaten to a bloody pulp on the floor. For Vito, that wasn't just an insult. It was a declaration. He demanded retribution.

It didn't come as fast as Vito wanted, but the score got settled. By the end of the year, Magnussen's body turned up in the St. Lawrence River, bound, gagged, and beaten to death.

Marty didn't just want to hold his turf. He wanted all of it. Sports betting. Coke pipelines. Meth labs. From Montreal to Ontario, then west to Alberta and B.C. He had the full blessing of Walter "Nurget" Stadnick, Canada's biker godfather, which meant Marty's moves weren't just personal. They were club policy.

"Nurget's a legend, and Marty wants to be one," said a source who knows both Stadnick and Marty. "And truth is, Marty's well on his way at this point in the game.

"Robert wouldn't be moving without Nurget's nod. Nurget sees Marty as the future and wants what Marty wants at the end, which is forwarding the interests of the club and making the club as big and influential as it can be in Canada.

"The Rizzutos are bleeding out. They have all kinds of exposure and blind spots in that organization. Nobody trusts anybody, power is decentralized or moving that way, to an extent, and Marty, like any great captain of industry or war general, wants to take advantage of it for himself and the *Hells*. He's playing it like a war general, like a captain of industry," the source said. "I don't think it's personal at all. It's strictly business, even if it's cold-hearted."

According to another source, Stadnick has been running interference for Marty with the Hells Angels' U.S. leadership. The Americans were worried the bad blood between the bikers and the Italians in Canada could spill south, poison million-dollar partnerships, and wreck the smooth flow of business across the border.

"The guys in the States thought they could get Marty to pull it back," the source said. "Nurget put a stop to that thinking real quick."

Sources say Stadnick isn't the only heavyweight backing Marty's push for dominance. In Ontario, *Les Hells'* power structure is marching in step with him. Two years ago, Robert even pulled Robert "Teflon Rob" Barletta into Montreal for reinforcements, a show of strength that rattled the streets.

The Ontario roster reads like a biker hall of fame. Joe Ertel and Joel "One-Eye J" Meyer run the province as president and vice president. Meyer once held the top spot himself before handing it off to "Joe E." Patrick Lock and Paul "Sasquatch" Porter call the shots in Ottawa. Martin "Burrito" Bernatchez and Philip "Crazy Phil" Boudreault hold the same titles for the Ontario Nomads.

Marty isn't just eyeing Montreal. Sources claim he's already plotting a move on mob rackets in Ontario once he's finished carving up Quebec's gambling and drug markets.

"All these guys in Ontario aren't territorial with Marty," said one source. "They welcome him in. They see him as the future."

But then, in early 2024, Leonardo made a move. He went north. Quebec City. There, he locked arms with a new kind of gangster, David "Pic" Turmel, a street-bred Canadian crime lord in his 30s who'd consolidated every serious drug crew in the city under his Blood Family Mafia banner. BFM didn't bow to anyone, especially not the Hells Angels chapter in Quebec City. Traditionally, the bikers taxed every gang 10% just for existing. Turmel told them to shove it up their ass.

With Leonardo's blessing, BFM became frontline muscle for the Rizzuto Mob in the war against the Hells Angels. That alliance also pulled in the Profit Boys, another ruthless Quebec City drug crew aligned with Turmel, and remnants of the Vikings Motorcycle Club, a former Hells Angels support club that had morphed into a hybrid biker-street-gang outfit now willing to turn their backs on the death head.

But alliances come with consequences.

Word on the street was that Marty put half a million dollars on Turmel's head, cash on the table for any Hells Angel in Europe willing to track him down and bury him.

The response was immediate. Sources on both sides of the law say Quebec City *Hells*, backed by a half-dozen lieutenants of gang boss Atna "2Pac" Onha, are already overseas, hunting Turmel across Europe. The contract is live, the money is real, and the clock is ticking.

"It's not going to end well for Pic," one criminal source said flatly. "Doesn't matter that the Rizzutos are behind him. The Hells Angels have thousands of killers in almost every country on the planet. The Rizzutos? They've got a few friends in Europe and South America. This isn't a fair fight. It's already game over."

Still, Leonardo was betting on chaos. He had no choice. Attrition had gutted his ranks, and street gangs were now his main soldiers. BFM, Profit Boys, and the Vikings riding in place of the bikers he'd once counted as blood brothers. The strategy was risky, maybe even suicidal, but in Montreal's underworld, survival has never been about playing safe.

This wasn't just about turf anymore. It was about rewriting the entire underworld's power map, one bullet, one body at a time.

By the fall of 2024, Montreal felt like a city on a fuse. The streets weren't just tense, they were tired. Blood had soaked into too many sidewalks, too many kitchen tiles, too many prison yards. The body count wasn't just a statistic anymore. It was a shadow hanging over everyone in the game.

Leonardo's side had scored small wins. Hits on mid-level bikers, seizures of drug shipments meant for HA channels, but Marty's war machine kept grinding forward. BFM lieutenants were getting picked off. Profit Boys were bleeding members. The Vikings MC, once loud about switching sides, were suddenly quieter, their clubhouse doors shut more often than open.

By November, the West End Gang, the city's Irish mob, stepped in. They weren't taking sides. They were playing referee. Through their boss, Kyle "K-Irish" Grabowski, whispers started moving. Enough was enough. Every bullet fired was bad for business. Coke was getting hung up at ports. Gambling money was drying up because bookies were too scared to answer phones.

Out of that pressure came *The Union*, a street-level enforcement and regulatory crew built from multiple street gangs. They weren't loyal to colors or flags. They answered only to the top table. The Rizzutos, the Hells Angels, and the West End Gang.

The Union wasn't just bikers and Sicilians. Arab crews had a seat. Black gang leaders had a stake. It was a stitched-together machine, designed to police the streets, tax the rackets, and keep chaos from burning the whole empire down.

Overseeing it all was Pietro "Black Pete" D'Adamo, the Rizzuto underboss. He was the point man for the triumvirate, the one making sure The Union served the interests of Montreal's three criminal superpowers.

The Union wasn't about friendship. It was about control, keeping the cash moving, the drugs flowing, and the peace, however fragile, enforced at gunpoint if necessary.

The groundwork for peace was there. All it needed was the right room, the right men, and the right moment.

That moment came on a freezing Monday night, December 11, 2024, at *Ristorante Da Emma* in downtown Montreal. The place was old-school stone walls, low lighting, the kind of joint where the pasta comes out steaming and the wine never stops pouring.

On one side of the table, you had Leonardo. Sharp suit, cool as ice, the last son of Montreal's most feared crime dynasty. He didn't need to say much. His name did the talking.

Right beside him was Pietro. He wasn't the guy you saw in the papers, but he was the guy who made the papers happen. Quiet, patient, the type who built meetings out of whispers and back channels. Every deal, every truce, every payoff, his fingerprints were there, even if nobody noticed.

D'Adamo wasn't just some button man, either. Back when Rocco Sollecito was alive, he was his right hand, the "Chief of Staff." These days, he ran the Southwest side for the Rizzutos, and he had another edge. He was sleeping with Leonardo's sister. That made him more than an adviser. That made him family.

And in this world, family meant everything.

Outside and inside the restaurant, Leonardo's security was everywhere, led by a man known only as "Happy," strategically posted to watch every door, every corner, every shadow.

On the other side of the table sat Marty. Montreal's Hells Angels boss. Big frame, sharp eyes, a grin that never told you if he was laughing with you or at you. Marty was the type who could crack a joke over coffee, then have you zipped in a trunk before dessert. That's why people feared him, because with Marty, you never knew when the switch was coming.

Next to him was Stéphane "Fess" Plouffe. Stone-faced, built for loyalty. If Marty was the mouth, Fess was the muscle. Orders didn't stay words with him. He turned them into reality. Cold, clean, no questions asked.

They didn't hug. They didn't shake hands right away. They sat. They drank. They ate. They talked.

And when they stood up, hours later, the war was over.

The groundwork for peace didn't come easy. It took two years of shootings, firebombs, and bodies in the street, old allies tearing each other apart for gambling, dope, and flesh in Quebec and Ontario.

Thing is, these crews weren't strangers. For decades, the Rizzutos, the Hells Angels, and the West End Gang ran the same rackets together. Sports books, backroom casinos, coke pipelines. They didn't just share profits. They shared blood on the streets.

The West Enders always had their grip on the waterfront, especially the docks. Port Authority, container yards, customs, if you wanted to move product through Quebec, you didn't do it without their nod. That's what made them valuable and dangerous.

The Sicilians and the bikers had buried the hatchet. They were back in business together, gambling, narcotics, sex rackets, all split and run like the old days. The streets would see less blood and more cash.

In January 2025, Pietro and Marty met again. This time, no cameras, no leaks. Just two men making sure the machinery they'd restarted kept humming.

But weeks later, the truce cracked again. For the second time, the Blood Family Mafia broke its word with the Hells Angels in Quebec City, still fighting over street tax. This time, it was Alex Maltais who almost paid the price. A Hells Angel with a target on his back, he dodged death when machine-gun fire ripped past him in a McDonald's parking lot on Vachon Boulevard. Broad daylight, grease and bullets flying.

That was it for the Leonardo. They pulled the plug, cut their ties to the BFM. Sources say it all came down to Turmel, the crew's fugitive boss. Even locked up in Rome, waiting on extradition for gangsterism and dope charges, Turmel refused to stand down. He wouldn't take orders, wouldn't bend. And in this world, that kind of defiance gets you isolated. Fast.

By the Spring of 2025, everybody knew it. The Rizzutos and the Hells Angels had kissed and made up. Allies again.

For now.

But in this city, peace doesn't mean the war is over. It just means the bodies aren't dropping today. Tomorrow's always up for grabs.

And sure enough, June 12 hit like a hammer. Leonardo, Stefano, and Pietro, dragged out in cuffs, lined up with eight others on murder charges. The cops had their ace in the hole, Frederick Silva. A hitter, a freelance killer who flipped in 2022 and started feeding them names.

That never would've flown back in the day. Not with the Sicilians. Not with the bikers. You had a beef, you handled it yourself. You didn't subcontract revenge. You didn't hire outsiders to pull your trigger.

But that's the new Montreal. The rules are bent, the codes are cracked, and the kings are either buried or caged.

The only thing that never changes? The street. The street remembers. The street waits.

# So, what now?

Digital and traditional crime are merging. Identity theft, ransomware, crypto laundering, it's all part of the portfolio. The mobster of tomorrow might never touch a gun but will move millions from a phone.

Canada's ports remain vulnerable. From Vancouver to Montreal, shipping containers are the veins of the drug trade. Corruption, understaffing, and loopholes are letting billions in product slip through.

Ethnic diversity is reshaping the game. Haitian, Arab, South Asian, and Latin American gangs are now power players. The old mafia monopoly is over.

Violence is precise, not flashy. Hits are clean. Messages are sent through bullet holes, not headlines.

The myths endure. The names Rizzuto and Boucher will never die, not in books, not in jailhouse whispers, not in the minds of young soldiers dreaming of a crown.

For nearly two decades, the alliance between the Rizzuto Family and the Hells Angels was criminal brilliance. A fusion of brains and brutality. A machine of money, murder, and silence.

But alliances forged in shadows rarely last in the light.

The brotherhood crumbled under its own weight. Betrayals. Egos. Blood feuds. What was once unity became suspicion. What was once an empire became a battleground.

Today, their legend still lingers in the streets of Montreal. But the game belongs to a new breed. Faster, colder, more connected. There are no more kings, just brokers, hustlers, killers, and codebreakers.

And the war never really ends.

Also, by Nicholas Anthony Parisi

Mafia Confession:
"King of Bootleggers" Murder

&

City of Betrayal:
The Genovese Family's Springfield Crew

"Like his other works, Parisi doesn't write from the outside looking in; he gives you the inside track, shaped by firsthand relationships, scars, and a lifetime inside the code."

Author Nick Parisi with Hells Angels legend Ralph "Sonny" Barger in San Bernardino, CA, circa 2010

# About the Author

Born in West Springfield, Massachusetts, Nick grew up surrounded by the real-life legends of organized crime. He didn't just study "The Families," he knew them. The names in his books aren't just subjects. They are family, friends, rivals, and mentors.

After relocating to California, Nick took a hard turn into the outlaw world, patching into one of the most notorious 1% motorcycle clubs in the nation. He didn't just ride, he climbed, eventually becoming a national officer and living the life most true crime writers only imagine.

Today, when he's not at the keyboard peeling back the layers of North America's criminal underworld, you'll find him on a golf course, fly fishing remote rivers, playing cards at a poker table, or chasing new stories across the globe.

**Parisi writes what he's lived, and he's lived what most wouldn't dare.**

www.ingramcontent.com/pod-product-compliance
Lightning Source LLC
Chambersburg PA
CBHW070615030426
42337CB00020B/3803